QUILTER'S ACADEMY

Vol. 4—Senior Year

A Skill-Building Course in Quiltmaking

Harriet Hargrave & Carrie Hargrave

C&T PUBLISHING

Text and Photography copyright © 2012 by Harriet Hargrave and Carrie Hargrave

Artwork copyright © 2012 by C&T Publishing, Inc.

Publisher: Amy Marson

Creative Director: Gailen Runge

Acquisitions Editor: Susanne Woods

Editor: Carrie Hargrave

Book Design Director: Kristen Yenche

Cover/Book Designer: Kerry Graham

Production Coordinator: Zinnia Heinzmann

Production Editor: Alice Mace Nakanishi

Illustrator: Wendy Mathson

Photography by Brian Birlauf unless otherwise noted

Published by C&T Publishing, Inc., P.O. Box 1456, Lafayette, CA 94549

Library of Congress Cataloging-in-Publication Data

Hargrave, Harriet.

Quilter's academy : a skill-building course in quiltmaking / by Harriet Hargrave and Carrie Hargrave.

p. cm.

ISBN 978-1-57120-594-0 (softcover)

1. Patchwork. 2. Quilting. I. Hargrave, Carrie, 1976- II. Title.

TT835.H3384 2009

746.46--dc22

2009008787

Printed in China

10 9 8 7 6 5 4 3 2 1

A Course in Quilting

A fresh new approach to uncovering the details that make quilting fun and rewarding. As we progress, you will be challenged to make stunning quilts using the skills achieved in earlier courses.

Quilting 401—Senior Year

Your senior year takes you into the most exciting of all designs—stars. We will explore stars made using 60° and 45° angles, as well as hexagons, Tumbling Blocks, Log Cabins, blocks with partial seams, and more. Drafting is a very large part of this process. Now you are ready to learn how to make those really stunning quilts you never thought you could!

Dedication

This book is dedicated to Carrie by Harriet. This mother could not be more proud of her daughter, who took on this project as a new quilter. Even though Carrie grew up in a quilt shop, her life was on a very different course until she decided to take over running the family business—a 30-year-old quilt shop. From learning basic precision in Volume 1 to the quilts in Volume 3, her piecing and quilting have improved by leaps and bounds. For someone who never wanted to be a quilter, she has surpassed my expectations and has made me very proud of her abilities. Don't think it has come naturally—many, many hours behind the machine doing things she really didn't want to do have paid off huge dividends in her skill level. We hope these books convince all the people out there who don't think they can do this—Carrie has proven that the processes throughout the books work!

—*Harriet*

The authors take full responsibility for the contents of this book, including the technical accuracy of the information. Please direct any questions to quilt.academy.q.a@earthlink.net. Please visit the Quilter's Academy blog, too, for additional information and discussions: quiltersacademy.blogspot.com.

Contents

Preface

You are holding the fourth in a series of six books. The purpose of the series is to build your quiltmaking skills on a firm foundation of basic skills, from beginner to advanced. Volume 1 laid the foundation for all of the successive books. If you have not worked through Volume 1 entirely, we *strongly* suggest that you do so first. These books are not all-inclusive. This fourth book relies on a more advanced set of skills to achieve the precision necessary to experience success with the patterns. We cover set-in piecing, Y-seam piecing, and partial seam piecing techniques, which require accurate sewing and extremely good pressing skills. If you run into any problems and have not worked through the entire series, we suggest that you stop and go back for "summer school," brush up your skills, and then try again. These quilts take time and patience; so don't try to hurry, falling back into shortcut techniques just to speed up.

 Introduction

If you have worked through the previous three volumes of *Quilter's Academy,* you have likely seen a vast improvement in your skill level. If you started as a new beginner, we are confident that you are experiencing the joy of having a toolbox of techniques that work and allow you to enjoy the process of quiltmaking.

We both remember our senior year in college as being the most fun of all four years of undergraduate work. The classes were challenging, allowing us to put into practice all the basics we had learned up to that point. The same is true with this series of courses. Volume 4 will put into practice the previous precision and drafting exercises you have learned up to now.

We are going to work with blocks and designs that utilize 45° and 60° diamonds, as well as hexagons, Log Cabin–type blocks, odd-shaped pieces, and more. As you progress through these classes, the blocks and techniques will get more difficult and time-consuming. We are starting with the 60° angles of hexagons and diamonds, as we feel they are the easiest to piece and a good warm-up to the more complicated 45° diamonds.

We have heard from many quilters over the course of the books' becoming available. They stated that even through they thought they were accomplished quiltmakers, they still learned a lot by working through each book in order. Each lesson in each of the books has been designed to be a skill builder, preparing you for the next, more difficult process.

Once you have mastered the concepts in Volume 4, you will be more than ready for Volume 5—*Medallion Quilts.* In Volume 5, everything from Volume 1 through Volume 4 will be put into play to teach you to design and construct a wide variety of borders, as well as your own original medallion quilts. For now, enjoy the adventure into diamonds and stars!

—*Harriet and Carrie*

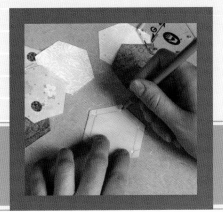

Class 410

Authors' note: We recommend that you make at least one block of every shape and pattern presented in the following lessons, just so you know the processes involved. We know these are not "quick and easy"; as you progress through the classes, each block will build on the previous one. If you skip hexagons or Tumbling Blocks because you don't care for them, you will likely run into some problems with the LeMoyne Star and Lone Star patterns. The skills in this book, as in the previous volumes, build on each other. We include some fun projects like placemats, table toppers, bed runners, and tea cozies to keep the projects small and doable, rather than overwhelming and time-consuming. The point is to learn the techniques, not spend weeks on each project. You will find that these are long-term projects, not "project in a weekend" style. Therefore, make sure you have extra yardage of all the fabrics you are using, especially background fabric. You never know when you will want to make something larger only to find the fabric is no longer available. We have also added quite a few illustrations of block and quilt designs for you to work with to spur ideas of your own. We really hope that you are starting to use your drafting and design skills to come up with your own original designs. Colored pencils can be your best friends. Use the worksheets in Volume 2 when you can to help place the blocks in different setting situations. Have fun creating!

LESSON ONE:

Introducing 60° angles—hexagons

We are starting with hexagons, as they are the base shape for 60° diamonds and are much easier to construct than 45° angles. Consider this a good warm-up for things to come. You might know this shape from the *Grandmother's Flower Garden* quilt that was so popular in the 1920s and 1930s.

It is also the gold standard of antique British quilts; the British are known for their hexagon quilts. The Japanese also excel at designing with hexagons.

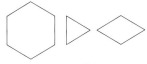 *note* If you haven't discovered the Japanese quilting magazines that are on the market, you might want to search them out. Look for Quilts Japan *and* Patchwork Quilt Tsushin. *The photography is beautiful, and there are many pages of quilting ideas illustrated from the featured quilts. These magazines are a true inspiration!*

The hexagon, equilateral triangle, and 60° diamond shapes below are all in the 60° family.

60° family of shapes

Where do these different shapes come from?

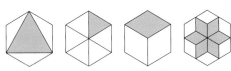

Different shapes derived from hexagons

The measurements for these shapes seem to have nothing in common with each other. If you measure from flat side to flat side, you get one measurement; if you measure from point to point, you get another.

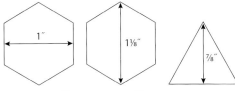

Measurements of hexagons

When designing with hexagons, you will find that they often fit together by using equilateral triangles and/or 60° diamonds. Cutting needs to be done very accurately. These shapes can be cut easily and accurately from strips using specific rulers. You will need to work with the finished measurement of one of the six sides of the hexagon. This is the one consistent measurement for all the pieces.

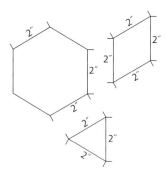

The one consistent measurement

note *The traditional way of describing the size of the hexagon relates to the measurement along one edge, not flat side to flat side or point to point. A 1" hexagon is actually 1" along each outside edge. If you want or need a 1" hexagon that finishes 1" from flat side to flat side, you will need to make your own template. The 1" (edge measurement) hexagon rulers and templates actually give you a 1¾" finished (flat side to flat side) hexagon.*

We prefer to work with templates when more than one shape is needed. Not only are they extremely accurate, but also the holes at the intersecting seamlines allow you to mark your starting and stopping points.

Perfect Patchwork Templates

In quilt designs, 60° diamonds are not as common as the 90° angle (squares and rectangles) or the 45° angle (half-square triangles and diamonds). Whereas the more common angles can be chain sewn, the 60° angle requires you to sew from seam allowance to seam allowance (also known as dot to dot), remove the piece from the machine, reposition it, and place it under the needle again. This slows down the sewing process considerably from the chain and strip piecing that you have experienced in the previous three volumes of *Quilter's Academy*.

The latest trend is to bypass set-in piecing when using hexagons or 60° diamonds. The unit is split in half, which allows the units to be sewn in rows with about half as many set-in corners. This technique has become common for the Tumbling Blocks pattern.

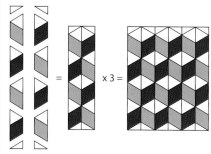

Seams through centers of hexagons

We have not added this system to the techniques presented here, as we feel it jeopardizes the integrity of the shape and is a real distraction to the eye when quilted. We also feel that it is no easier to piece than a Y-seam, and it makes all seam allowances and points meet in a straight seam. If you want to pursue this method, visit your local quilt shop, where you are apt to find patterns with this process featured.

You will also discover that when the size of the hexagons gets small, it is difficult to work with them under the foot of the sewing machine. There are times when working over paper is the easiest method for working with small units. We address a machine-stitching method for achieving English paper piecing in Lesson Six.

Now is a good time in your quilt-making venture to slow down and enjoy the process of set-in piecing. You will find most quilters do not attempt these patterns anymore, so when you are successful, you will find admiration coming your way for your perseverance!

LESSON TWO:
Basic drafting

Before we start to draft hexagons, gather up the following list of basic drafting tools that you will need throughout this book.

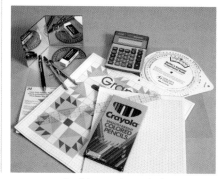

Drafting tools needed

* Sheets of isometric graph paper for designing with 60° shapes, such as equilateral triangles, hexagons, and diamonds

* .05 mechanical pencil—Use hard lead to prevent smearing.

* Colored pencils

* Erasers—Staedtler Mars plastic is recommended.

* Drafting ruler—There are many on the market. A good choice is a thin metal ruler with cork on the back. If you prefer plastic, C-Thru makes a thin drafting ruler that is easy to read and see-through for line placement. Do not use your thick rotary rulers for drafting, as the lines are too wide for accurate measuring.

* Compass—Be sure you upgrade from the one you had in grade school. A compass with a threaded crossbar will hold the setting you set. If you need a large circle, there is a product known as a yardstick compass that attaches to a yardstick.

* Protractor—Use to measure and mark angles.

* Calculator

* Proportional scale—This tool allows you to determine how much to enlarge or reduce any block you are designing.

* Extra-thick template plastic for templates

* 2 – 4″ or 6″ mirrors, taped together on one edge

We will start the drafting process with the simplest method, so all you need right now is graph paper and a compass.

1. Using a sheet of graph paper larger than the size hexagon you want, draw a square on the paper that is the desired size for the hexagon. The size of the square—side to side—will be referred to as "X."

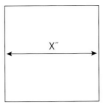

Draw a square on graph paper.

2. Divide the square in half both vertically and horizontally to find the center. You can either measure the square or fold the paper in half to establish a center point. Adjust your compass so that it is the length from the center to the side of the square. This is the radius of the circle. Draw a circle.

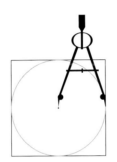

Use compass to draw circle.

3. Using the same compass setting, place the point of the compass on the circle where it intersects the horizontal center line and make a mark along the circle. Move the point of the compass to the mark just drawn and make a second mark along the circle. Continue around the circle until you arrive back where you started. You should have 6 marks around the circle that divide it evenly.

Measure and mark 6 divisions.

4. Use a ruler and draw straight lines around the circle to connect the marks. This basic hexagon shape

can then be divided in any of the numerous ways shown on page 5.

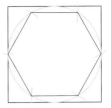

Connect marks with straight lines.

LESSON THREE:
Review of the basics

Following is a list of the basic piecing principles that we covered in detail in Volumes 1 and 2. If you haven't read and worked through these critical volumes, please take the time to review them before starting this course. The projects in this volume rely on your ability to sew an accurate seam and to press to take control of the seam allowances. We will no longer be cutting a little large to trim for extreme accuracy. Many of the projects rely on accurate, exact-size cutting and working with templates. If your accuracy is not spot-on, you will likely experience frustration and points that are missing.

* Always work on the straight grain, either lengthwise or crosswise. Be sure that you have torn both ends of your yardage and have realigned the crosswise grain of all the pieces before you begin to cut. Volume 1, Class 120, Lesson Three (pages 16 and 17)

* Accurate cutting is the beginning of your success or frustration as you piece. Be sure to use the correct ruler for the job. You need to commit to a single brand of rulers (unless they are specialty rulers for different shapes) that you can easily read to maintain accuracy. Volume 1, Class 120, Lessons Four and Five (pages 17–19)

❋ Find your personal accurate seam allowances. Remember that ¼" seam allowances don't work but scant ¼" seam allowances do. This will never be more evident than when you begin to sew 60° angles. Set up a system on your machine that allows you to have accurate finished units, not perfect ¼" seam allowances. This will be a critical point for the set-in piecing you will be doing in these classes. Volume 1, Class 130, Lessons One and Two (pages 20–23)

❋ Pressing can make or break your quilt top. Therefore, it is one of the most important processes to master. Proper pressing leads to flat, straight, extremely accurate pieced tops. If you are still working on a standard ironing board, now might be the time to invest in a Big Board or similar product. A high-quality iron, such as the Reliable Digital Velocity, is also helpful when pressing. Volume 1, Class 130, Lesson Four (page 26)

❋ Measure for accuracy. After you sew and press each seam, align a ruler on the seam and check that the unit measurement from the seam to the raw edge is exact. This prevents all the small distortions that occur when cutting, sewing, and pressing. Volume 1, Class 130, Lesson Five (page 27)

❋ Always start with a well-cleaned and oiled machine. Volume 2, Class 210, Lesson Two (pages 6–14)

❋ Sew samples with the fabrics you are going to be using to check for thread tension problems. Volume 2, Class 210, Lesson Two (page 11)

❋ Always start with a new sewing machine needle and have the one that is best suited for the type of sewing you will be doing and the thread size and type you are using. Volume 2, Class 210, Lesson Two (pages 12–14)

❋ Always test dark, rich colors for colorfastness. Volume 2, Class 220, Lesson Two (pages 17–20)

> **tip**
>
> Two of the most important considerations that we address over and over in Volumes 1 and 2 are thread weight and seam allowances. If you are still having problems with accuracy at this time, stop and master these concepts before you attempt any of the processes in this book. A correct seam allowance takes time and patience to master, as ¼" is not what you want to be sewing; it is the amount that is taken out of the piece with each seam sewn. The first consideration is the weight of thread you are using. All of our piecing is done with Presencia 60/3 sewing thread. This thread is fine and strong, 100% Egyptian cotton, and, in our opinion, the very best piecing thread on the market. The accuracy we achieve in our piecing is to a great part attributable to this thread and a size 70/10 needle. The thicker the thread, the more space it takes up in the seam, causing the finished unit to shrink. For the piecing in this book, 50/3 sewing thread is a bit too heavy.
>
> The second consideration is your seam allowance measurement. You need to allow for the thickness of the thread *and* the bend of the fabric created when you press the seam allowances to one side or open. To compensate for these two situations, a *scant* ¼" is necessary. If this is new to you and you have not worked through Volume 1, please take the time to go back and get a correct seam allowance for your machine (Volume 1, Class 130, Lessons One and Two, pages 20–23). It would be better to have this mastered now than deal with the aggravation of sewing and ripping when the angles used in this book don't fit together properly.

LESSON FOUR:
Piecing basic hexagons

Probably the most notable design using hexagons is the *Grandmother's Flower Garden* or variations on that theme. These patterns use only hexagon shapes, sewn side by side, to create the design. Color placement is very important to the design.

HELPFUL TOOLS FOR CUTTING AND SEWING 60° SHAPES

At the very least, you are going to need a rotary ruler with 60° and 45° lines. We find that many of the rulers have the lines, but their placement on the ruler is not always where we would like them to be. There are numerous specialty rulers designed specifically for working with these angles. If you already have rulers that you like to work with, start there. However, if you want to try to simplify the cutting and achieve the greatest accuracy, look for any of the following rulers or templates at your local quilt shop.

❋ Creative Grids 60° Triangle Ruler

❋ Perfect Patchwork Templates, Sets G and H, from Marti Michell

❄ Easy Six, by Sharon Hultgren (EZ International brand), designed to make quick and accurate six-pointed stars, Tumbling Blocks, and 60° diamonds.

❄ Easy Hexagon, by Sharon Hultgren, designed for quick and accurate cutting of hexagons accommodating 1″–3″ finished sizes in ½″ increments

❄ Easy Three, by Sharon Hultgren, used when cutting equal-sided triangles from strips (used in six-pointed stars)

❄ My Favorite Hexagon Ruler from Marti Michell

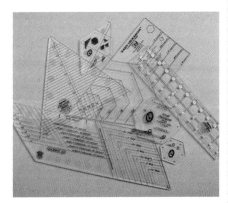

Various rulers

If you have drafted your pattern to a size that is not on one of the rulers or a precut template (say you want a 2¼″ finished hexagon), you can create your own templates from graph paper, sandpaper, and extra-heavy template plastic. (Refer to Volume 3, Class 350, Lesson One, page 68.)

We also recommend that you use Clover Patchwork Pins for the construction of these pieces. You will need to pin at the ends of seams, and these are the finest pins available. They do not cause distortion of the layers and can be sewn over if you sew slowly—which is a given with set-in piecing.

GETTING READY TO SEW

Now that you have your tools gathered up, it is time to get ready to learn how to piece hexagons. Once your fabric is straightened, trim off one end to get a perfect 90° cut to the double fold. To determine the strip width you need, measure your template or drafted pattern from flat side to flat side. *Be sure seam allowances are added!* If you are working with commercial templates or specialty rulers, the seam allowances are generally included. Because the first project uses only hexagons, you might want to work with the EZ International Easy Hexagon ruler. It offers five different sizes on one ruler, starting with 1″ and growing by ½″ up to 3″ hexagons. Remember, this measurement refers to each side of the hexagon, not the finished size. The Easy Hexagon ruler also has an elongated end that is used to cut the strip to the needed width and makes it very easy to visually check against the hexagon shape on the ruler. One ruler does both jobs. The instructions on the ruler package will walk you through how to use it to cut various sizes of hexagons.

Once the cutting is finished, mark the seamlines along the cut edges of each piece. At the very least, mark a dot at each intersection. This is really important, as you don't want to sew past the seam intersections when sewing pieces together. If you have a set of Perfect Patchwork Templates with hexagons (Set G or H), the holes in the templates are positioned for this purpose. You can also make your own marking template by cutting a stencil the cut size of the hexagon and, using a ¹⁄₁₆″ hole punch, making a hole

where the lines intersect. The hexagons are now ready to piece together.

Marking dots with template—both homemade and Perfect Patchwork

Get your machine ready for sewing by making sure it is clean and oiled. Use a new needle that is appropriate for the thread you are using. We use Presencia 60/3 exclusively when piecing because of its fineness and lack of lint. We use a 70/10 universal needle with this thread. The finer the needle, the easier it will be to start and stop the stitching in such limited areas. Set your stitch length at 2.0. Most machines default to a 2.5 stitch length (about 10 stitches per inch), which is too long for this technique. Using the Perkins Dry Goods ruler, graph paper, or whatever method you use to gauge your perfect seam allowance, find your scant ¼″ seam allowance and use a thick piece of ¼″ masking tape as a barrier seam guide or use your guide of choice. We use the Bernina #13 foot with the guide attached. You want to set up to sew as accurately as you can.

Y-SEAMS (SET-IN PIECING)

Set-in piecing, also known as sewing Y-seams, is a process that seems to make quilters want to run for the hills! It is commonly thought that this type of piecing is difficult. We wouldn't call if difficult at this stage of *Quilter's Academy* if you have worked through the previous three volumes; it's just time-consuming. We plan to walk you through the techniques that make this process much less painful to get you excited about the prospect of being able to make the wonderful designs that use the 60° and 45° angles that require Y-seams.

We tried several different approaches to piecing hexagons before writing these instructions. We have chosen the one that we think is the most straightforward and the easiest for you to be successful. We hope you agree. We suggest that you cut a few hexagons to experience the process before starting one of the projects. To make a single Grandmother's Flower Garden flower, cut one hexagon for the center and six hexagons for the first round. Draft the hexagon inside a 2½″ square. These units will be large enough to handle easily your first time out.

We also suggest that you pay special attention to the grainline of the hexagon units. Two edges of the hexagon are on the straight grain—the flat side–to–flat side direction. The opposite grainline runs point to point, making the remaining four points slightly bias. You might want to lightly mark the grain on the backsides of your pieces until you are comfortable determining which edges are straight. It is always easier to see the grain on the backside of the fabric.

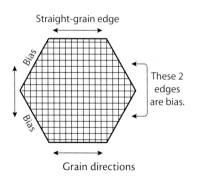
Grain directions

When laying out the hexagons to develop the pattern, work with the grain of each for proper placement. The straight-grain edge of each of the Round 1 pieces will go next to the center unit. As the pieces radiate out, the bias edges will nest between the two hexagons. This will make more sense when you actually are sewing the units together. Refer to the illustration below if you get confused.

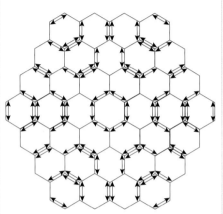
Grain position for each hexagon within block

Before sewing, lay out the blocks near your machine where they will not be in the way of your sewing so you can plan the grain placement as illustrated. The first seam will be the center unit and one side unit, with straight-grain sides of the hexagons next to one another. Start your stitching at the dot with a few very small stitches or use the lock stitch (also called tack or fix stitch) built into your machine. Elongate the stitch to 2.0 and continue the seam to the next dot. Just before you get to the dot, reduce the stitch length, or use the lock stitch, to secure the end of the seam. Trim your threads.

First two hexagons joined

You will not be pressing after every seam during construction. The hexagons are going to alternate as you go around the center. Once the first one is added to the center, skip one edge of the center and add a second hexagon. Again, skip an edge and add a third. These seams can now be carefully pressed toward the Round 1 hexagons. You are only sewing the seam that connects the unit to the center at this time.

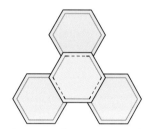
Three hexagons alternated around center

Once the first three are pressed, add the remaining three hexagons. If you were accurate when adding the first three, the dots on the remaining hexagons will lie exactly on top of the pressed seam allowance on each end of the new seam. Pin in place and then stitch dot to dot. We like to position the hexagon being added face up for placement; then we flip the unit over so that we can see the previously sewn seams. It is more accurate if you can start and stop exactly at the previous stitching. Once stitched, press these seams toward the center.

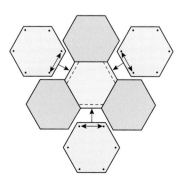
Six hexagons added to center

The next step is to stitch the sides together. Fold the unit in half and align the edges of two hexagons. Pull the seam allowance free of any other piece to prevent sewing in another free edge. Stitch dot to dot, making tiny stitches at each dot. Be careful not to stitch beyond the previous stitching. Continue around the center until all the seams of the first round have been joined.

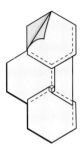

Aligning seams

The pressing is much like that for fanned seams that you learned in Volume 1, Class 150 (page 58), but this time the seams spin instead of fan. As for Four-Patch and Nine-Patch blocks, this method reduces the bulk where the seam allowances meet. To create the spin, the seam allowances will again alternate. On one hexagon, both side seam allowances will be pressed onto one hexagon. On the next, they will point away from each other. Examine the following illustration and photo to see how the seam allowances are pressed.

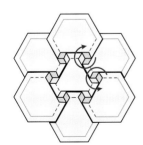

Direction of seam allowances to obtain spin at intersections

Back of sample

When you have a pattern that calls for another round of hexagons, the same process of alternating units is used. Start by positioning a hexagon for the second round with the bias points fitting into the space between two Round 1 hexagons. This time you will sew two sides of the hexagon in place. Position the hexagon, matching the dots, with the pressed seams and the new hexagon on top. You will sew the seam that joins the new hexagon onto the one from Round 1 first. Once it is in place and pinned, turn it over and position it for stitching. Stitch from seam to seam (dot to dot). Once you reach the dot, shorten the stitch length. Turn the hexagon to align the next seam. Fold the unit back and align the edges exactly. Pin and stitch from dot to dot. When you turn the piece to the front, the point should lie perfectly flat. Continue adding five more hexagons, alternating them around the edge.

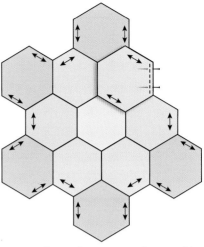

Inserting first six hexagons, sewing two sides

You have three seams to join when you add the last six hexagons. Stitch the straight-grain side to the Round 1 hexagon; then stitch the remaining two sides. Continue until all twelve hexagons are in place. Again, spin the seams and press well from the front.

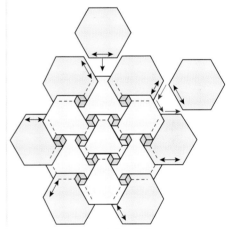

Inserting remaining six hexagons, sewing three seams

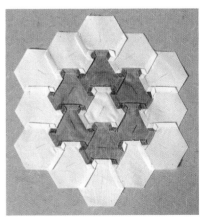

Back of block with two rounds

You have now experienced the basics of set-in piecing and probably found it a bit more time-consuming than you thought it would be. However, the process picks up speed once you get the sewing order and pressing directions into a system. Are you ready for more? Now let's look at some of the fun ideas you can turn into stunning quilts.

Designing with 60° angles

We have found these little pieces to be quite addicting. There are endless ways to color hexagons to get patterns and designs. Following are nine stunning patterns that use hexagons only. They are round, oval, and colored to look like stars. Using the hexagon graph paper at the end of this chapter, see how many different patterns you can create by coloring in the shapes. You might want to consider making one of these now that you have learned the process, or use any of them as a jumping-off place for bigger and better ideas.

As you work with different designs, you will find that sometimes the hexagons sit on a flat side and other times they stand on point. This can affect the shape and size of the design.

Nine ideas for color placement and shape using only hexagons

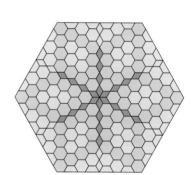

Adding diamonds to star design

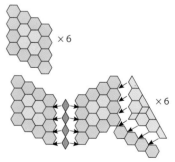

× 6

× 6

Breakout of star units for construction

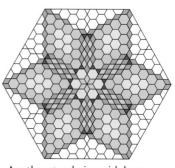

Another star design with hexagons and diamonds

LESSON SIX:

English paper piecing by machine

Paper piecing hexagons has been the standard way of working with this shape for generations. Heavy paper is cut into the hexagon shape, fabric is folded over the edges, and then the folded edges are matched together and hand stitched. Great accuracy is achieved, and all pressing is eliminated. This method makes the piecing very portable. As we were playing with the paper piecing process, we came up with a method that allows prepared hexagon pieces to be stitched on the machine. We found that it is fairly easy to piece hexagons that are at least 1½″ on the machine, but anything smaller is more than tedious and very difficult to manipulate under the presser foot and to press accurately. Therefore, we present a process of sewing small, prepared pieces on the machine for accuracy and to avoid the need for pressing.

tip We suggest that you purchase precut hexagon papers for this process. They are die-cut and very accurate. A couple of brands you might look for are Paper Pieces (www.paperpieces.com) and Patchwork with Busy Fingers (www.busyfingerspatchwork.com). Just remember, like the rulers and templates, the 1″ paper does not give you a 1″ hexagon. If you need the flat side–to–flat side measurement to be a specific size, you will need to draft your own hexagon and cut your own papers.

Cut squares of fabric ½″ larger than the paper pieces. Pin the paper onto the fabric square. Cut around the paper, leaving a scant ¼″ seam allowance on all sides.

You can either thread baste the seam allowance over to the back on all sides or use a fabric-basting gluestick to lightly glue the seam allowances over to the back. If you thread baste, you can easily take out the stitches after all the pieces are joined. You will find it is faster in the beginning to use a gluestick, but make sure to use a very small amount of glue just along the edge of the paper. If too much glue is used, you will need to lightly dampen the pieces on the back to dissolve the glue before removing the papers. We prefer a glue pen to a gluestick, as the glue is drier and easier to control on the edges of the papers. It's your choice as to which method you prefer.

If you choose to glue, start by gluing the opposite sides that are on the straight grain of the fabric. Apply a very light line of glue on the edge of the paper and fold over the seam allowance, making sure the fabric is snug on the paper. Proceed to the seam allowances that are on either side of the first glued sides, making sure the corners are secure and the edges are tight.

The stitch that we use on our machines (older Berninas) is called a gathering stitch. It is used to sew over cord for gathering, to sew shirring elastic, or to join seams that have seam allowances pressed over and butted together. It is often used for swimsuit fabrics, which is what gave Harriet the idea to use the stitch to join the covered pieces.

Gathering stitch

Start by making a sample using invisible nylon thread in the top of the machine and a very fine 60/2 machine embroidery thread in the bobbin. Another option is 100/2 silk in both the top and bottom in a very neutral color that blends into the fabric. A 60/8 universal sewing machine needle is needed for this process. With these threads, this stitch becomes completely invisible on the top. We suggest you sew a few samples to get the tension correct so you do not see anything on the tops of the pieces. Set your stitches so that the zigzag swings over just enough to catch one or two threads of the fabric on each side of the joined edges. When the needle goes back to the center, it needs to be in the ditch, where the two pieces are butted together. We set our machine at 1 width and ½ length and reduced the top tension from 5 to 3.

Threads, needles, and paper shapes

Starting with the center unit, position one petal against the center and stitch it in place.

Stitching first two units

Position the second petal next to the center and the first petal. Stitch between the two petals and then the center, pivoting at the intersection.

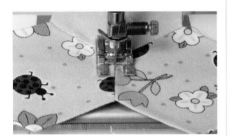
Adding third piece

Continue adding petals around the center. When you get to the sixth unit, you will have three sides to stitch.

Adding last piece

Continue this process until all the units of your project are joined. We suggest that if you choose this method for a large project, you work in smaller sections and join them at the end. It will be less bulky than manipulating a large piece through the machine.

If you glued the seam allowances, the papers should pop out easily if you used minimal glue. If they do not come out easily, *very lightly* dampen

the seam allowances from the backside. The glue will soften and release from the paper. The zigzag stitch is so narrow, the paper will pop out easily. Do not use too much water! With an iron heated to *no hotter than the wool setting*, press the seam allowances flat on the back. Again, it is easiest to work in small sections when removing the paper.

If you basted the seam allowances, pull on the knot you made in the

basting thread from the back and gently pull it out of each piece. Press if necessary.

Close-up of joined hexagons

Hexagon projects

PROJECT ONE: PAPER-PIECED *TEATIME* PLACEMAT AND TEA COZY

Teatime

Placemat size: 15″ × 19″

Tea cozy size: 12″ × 10″

Hexagon size: 1¼″ finished

Hexagons needed: 170 for both placemats and 70 for tea cozy

Yardages needed:

　Scrap of yellow

　⅛ yard medium purple floral

　¼ yard medium lavender tonal

　⅓ yard light purple print

　⅓ yard medium green tonal

　¼ yard medium green floral

　⅛ yard each of four additional purples—a medium dark purple, a lavender, a medium light purple, and a light lavender

　⅛ yard each of four additional greens—a dark medium green, two light medium greens, and a light green

For this fun project, Carrie chose to work with 1¼″ precut hexagon papers from Paper Pieces. Precut each fabric into 2¾″ × 3⅛″ rectangles to help make cutting the individual hexagons easier. Start by straightening your fabric and then cutting the fabric into 2¾″-wide strips. You will get 13 rectangles per strip.

Following is the number of hexagons of each color required to complete this project:

❋ 2 yellow—both for placemats

❋ 21 medium purple floral—16 for placemats, 5 for tea cozy

❋ 37 medium lavender tonal—32 for placemats, 5 for tea cozy

❋ 49 light purple print—44 for placemats, 5 for tea cozy

❋ 49 medium green tonal—44 for placemats, 5 for tea cozy

❋ 38 medium green floral—32 for placemats, 6 for tea cozy

❋ 6 medium dark purple—for tea cozy

❋ 5 lavender—for tea cozy

❋ 5 medium light purple—for tea cozy

❋ 5 light lavender—for tea cozy

❋ 5 dark medium green—for tea cozy

❋ 6 light medium green—for tea cozy

❋ 6 light green—for tea cozy

❋ 6 very light green—for tea cozy

You will need 240 hexagon papers to complete this project.

Once all the fabric is cut into rectangles, trim the rectangles to fit the hexagon papers. Center the hexagon papers on the fabric. Carefully turn the edges of the fabric over the paper and secure with a gluestick or glue pen, making sure that the edges are crisp, clean, and tight against the paper.

Set up your machine with either 100/2 silk thread that matches the color of your hexagons or invisible nylon thread. Set the stitch to the gathering stitch as discussed previously (page 13), with the recommended stitch length and width. You may want to prepare a couple of extra hexagons to practice the stitch to make sure you know where you are looking when stitching the hexagons together, as well as making sure that your stitch length and width setting are the appropriate size.

To begin constructing the placemat, lay the center yellow hexagon down and place a medium purple floral hexagon next to it; stitch together.

Place the next hexagon beside the purple hexagon you just sewed on and sew the two floral hexagons together, pivoting at the corner. Sew the second floral hexagon to the yellow center. Continue this way until all six hexagons are attached to the center yellow. On the sixth hexagon, sew on all three sides that abut on the final hexagon to complete the round. (Refer to the photo on page 14.)

Next, add the remaining two hexagons of the purple floral to begin the diamond shape. Place one hexagon in the crotch of the purple floral hexagon round and sew the two sides. Repeat on the exact opposite side of the round.

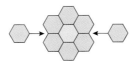

Creating diamond shape on first round

To speed things up for the next round, you can create "rows" of hexagons

using the medium lavender tonal. Construct two rows of four hexagons each and two rows of three hexagons each simply by sewing each flat side to the next hexagon until you have rows of four or three. You will have two extra single hexagons for each placemat that you will need later.

Creating rows of four hexagons

Attach the rows you just created. Start with a row of three. Nest this row next to the round already sewn, placing the first hexagon in the row on the top right edge of the last hexagon you attached.

Placement of rows of three hexagons

The row should fall in place down the side of the center diamond. Starting at the top point of the row where it touches the center diamond, sew and attach the row to the center diamond. Sew the five edges that are in contact with the center. Repeat this for the other row of three, placing it in the exact opposite side of the center diamond.

Once these two row sets are attached, you can see where the two rows of four need to be placed. This time, once you get the row of four butted up to the center, you are on the left side of the last hexagon of the center round. You have eight edges to sew to attach this row, not only to the center but also to the ends of the rows of three.

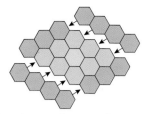

Attachment placement for rows of
four hexagons for Round 2

As with the first round of purple, you will have two extra hexagons per placemat left over. A single hexagon needs to be added to each end, as you did for the center, to continue the diamond shape.

For the third round of purple hexagons, construct two rows of five hexagons and two rows of six hexagons and attach these exactly as you did with Round 2.

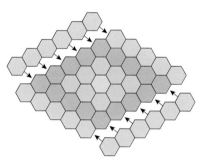

Attachment placement for Round 3

Once you have Round 3 sewn on, switch the thread color if you are using silk thread in the top of your sewing machine.

To create the first green round (Round 4 of the placemat), sew together two rows of five hexagons and two rows of six hexagons of the medium green tonal. Then make four rows of three hexagons of the medium green floral. Sew these row sets together as shown.

Sewing green row sets together

Now add the four single medium green floral hexagons to make the "corners" of these sections.

Attaching last hexagon to green corners

If you are not using nylon thread in the top of your machine, determine which color will hide the best between the two colors where the green and purple meet. Attach the green corner rounds to your purple diamond. On the rows of five hexagons, you will have ten edges to sew, and on the rows of six hexagons, you will have twelve edges to attach.

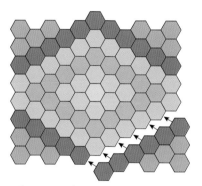

Placement of green corner rounds on
purple diamond

And that's it. You have the first placemat completed. Repeat the process to make the second placemat, and then on to the tea cozy.

This simple tea cozy is made up of two panels of random-colored hexagons of the same colors as the placemats.

If you haven't already covered all your hexagon papers for the tea cozy, do that now. You will need a total of 70 hexagons—34 of six different greens and 36 of seven different lavenders and purples.

The tea cozy is made by first creating rows and then attaching the rows to each other.

The following diagram shows the color placement in each of the six rows for each of the two panels of the tea cozy.

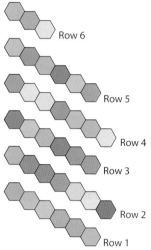

Row 6
Row 5
Row 4
Row 3
Row 2
Row 1

Tea cozy panel row layout

Sew the hexagons in each row together and then attach the rows to each other as shown in the diagram on page 17.

Once you have the panels for the tea cozy completed, as well as the two placemats, you will need to remove the papers. The easiest way to accomplish this is to lightly spray the backside of each item with water (one item at a time) to loosen the glue. Gently lift the turned seam allowance off the paper and pull the paper away from the fabric and stitching. From the wrong side of each item, with your iron set on wool, press the seam allowances back in place.

Next, mark the placemat for quilting. Layer it with a thin, low-shrinkage batting and quilt it. Once the placemats are quilted, trim them to 15½″ × 19½″. Carrie chose to round the corners of her placemats. This can easily be done by lining up the edge of your ruler with the inside points of the hexagons and drawing a straight line with a blue washaway marker. Do this on all four sides of the placemats. Then, using either a French curve or a round object with a 4″ diameter, slide the curve into the corners until it touches both straight lines. Trace the curve and then trim it with scissors, making sure you have a smooth transition from the straight edges of the top and bottom to the curved corners. If you have chosen to have rounded corners on your placemats, you also need to make bias binding in order to have the binding lie nicely. Follow the instructions in Lesson Two of Class 490 (page 122) to cut the bias strips for the binding.

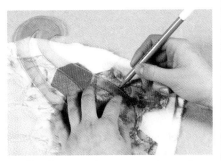

Creating curved corners on placemats

To complete the tea cozy, remove the papers from each of the panels and then press the seam allowances flat. Then mark, layer, and quilt the two panels.

Using a homemade compass from a 9½″ piece of string tied to a pencil, locate the very center of the bottom row of each tea cozy panel. Hold the string at this center point; with the pencil, draw a light line in an arc from the bottom left side of each panel across the top to the bottom right side of each panel. You can also use a Flexicurve to determine and mark the curve. This tool is a flexible ruler that can be formed to any shape needed.

Marking arc on tea cozy panel with homemade compass

Marking arc on tea cozy panel with Flexicurve

Once you have the arc marked, trim the tea cozy along this line. Then, just as you did for the placemats, line up your ruler with the inside points of the hexagons on the bottom edge and mark a line. Then cut off the extra fabric. Once your tea cozy halves are trimmed, fold a panel in half and mark the exact center of the top of the panel. Measure 1½″ down from this mark and make a second mark. Measure ¾″ on each side of the top mark and make a third and fourth mark at these locations. Now draw a line connecting these two new marks with the second mark you made 1½″ down.

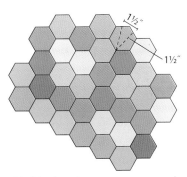

Marking locations on tea cozy panel

Cut out the wedge that you just marked to create the dart that will shape your tea cozy so that it will fit nicely over your teapot. Starting at the top mark on the right, cut down to the second mark; then go back to the top left mark and cut down. This should free the small wedge from the panel. Once you have done this on both panels, it is time to construct your tea cozy.

With the hexagon sides (right sides) together and using a ½″ seam allowance, sew the two panels together, skipping over the open wedge area that you just cut out. Press the seam allowance on each side of the wedge out in opposite directions.

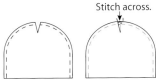

Stitching tea cozy halves together

Next, reorient the two panels so that you can sew the wedge seam. Make sure that you butt the seam allowances together; pin and then sew from the very edge of the panel, still with a ½″ seam allowance, to the other side. That's nearly it!

Turn the tea cozy right side out and bind. Unlike for the placemats, you can make normal straight binding for the bottom of the tea cozy. Bind the bottom edge, wash out your quilt markings, and add a fun tassel or pom-pom to the top of your tea cozy for easy grasping. And you are done! Time for tea! Enjoy!

PROJECT TWO: *MOSAIC STAR*

Mosaic Star

Quilt top size: approximately 50″ corner to corner

Hexagon size: 1″ finished

Hexagons needed: 631

Yardages needed:

At a minimum, you will need 22 different colors to create this table topper quilt. If you choose to use a different fabric in each design element, you will need 34 different colors. The yardages given below are for the 22-color option.*

　1⅓ yards cream background

　⅙ yard each of 6 different colors for outer border and Round 1 of Grandmother's Flower Garden units

　⅛ yard each of 6 colors for outer rounds of Grandmother's Flower Garden units

　Scraps of 7 different fabrics for centers of Grandmother's Flower Garden units, for very center of star, and for star point centers on border

　⅛ yard fabric for Round 1 in star center

　⅙ yard fabric for 18 pieces in middle of center star

　¼ yard of main color that creates star

* The fabric yardages given above are only a minimum guideline. If you choose a fabric that can be fussy cut to center an element within each hexagon, you may need to add half again the yardage given or more.

For this project, Carrie chose to work with Marti Michell's template #46 from Perfect Patchwork Templates, Set G. Precut each fabric into 2¼″ × 2⅝″

rectangles to make preparation easier. Start by straightening your fabric and then cutting it into 2¼″-wide strips. Doing this will yield 16 rectangles per strip.

Once you cut the rectangles, layer four rectangles at a time, position template #46 on top, and cut around the template. You may want to alternate the cutting process with the marking of the dots on your fabric so that you do not get too overwhelmed with the sheer number of hexagons you need to cut and mark for this project.

note As Carrie was marking the dots on the backsides of her different fabrics, she experimented with a number of different marking tools and came to the following conclusions:

On fabrics that had more print or a darker-colored back, a black Pigma Micron pen size #05 was the easiest to see. On lighter-colored fabrics or fabrics that had less print, a fine-line washaway marker was the easiest to see. You may want to start here, but if you still have trouble seeing the dots, do not hesitate to try other marking tools. Just be careful of markers not made to mark fabric, as they may be permanent and bleed through the fabric, creating an unsightly mark on the front of your quilt top.

Follow the basic instructions for joining hexagons (page 10).

At times, you might sew a row of hexagons together instead of working in the round. If this is the case, be sure to lay out the next row to be attached next to the quilt top to check the orientation. Flip the row over the quilt top, align the two edges to be sewn together, and sew dot to dot. Stop, cut your thread, and realign the row with the next edge of the quilt top to be sewn. Align all edges and again sew dot to dot. You will soon find a rhythm in doing this, making the assembly of your quilt top go faster.

Step 1 of attaching row
to other quilt elements

Step 2 of attaching row
to other quilt elements

Step 3 of attaching row
to other quilt elements

After many fits and starts, Carrie finally found a relatively easy way to construct the elements of this quilt top so they could be put together with a minimum of difficulty.

Refer to the following set of illustrations to see the different elements Carrie identified for ease of construction.

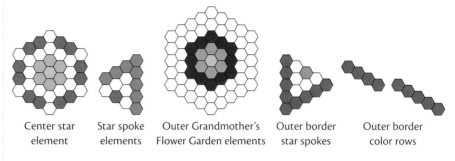

Center star
element

Star spoke
elements

Outer Grandmother's
Flower Garden elements

Outer border
star spokes

Outer border
color rows

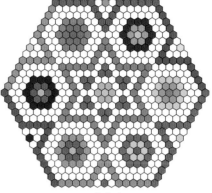

Layout of all elements

Remember to slow down, relax, and enjoy the process of making this project. This will be one of the most time-consuming projects that you will encounter in this book. But when it is said and done, you will have created a masterpiece in about one-tenth the time it would take to do this same project by hand. So again, take your time and just enjoy the process; walk away, if necessary, if you get tired or frustrated. This is supposed to be fun. Remember, you are creating an heirloom, and it is well worth the effort and attention to detail.

Class 420

LESSON ONE:

Basic construction of Tumbling Blocks

DIMENSION CREATED BY 60° DIAMONDS

Now that you have mastered setting in short seams, it is time to move on to Tumbling Blocks—a pattern that is created when three 60°diamonds are sewn together to make a hexagon. Set-in seams are needed where the three units converge. The 60° angle not only creates hexagons but also has the fun characteristic of being able to produce a three-dimensional effect with the use of color and value. Architects use many 60° angles to create the three-dimensional illusion when drawing buildings. This is known as isometric drawing.

Tumbling Blocks, also known as Baby Blocks

Tumbling Blocks is a traditional pattern well known to quilters. It is intriguing because of all the possibilities it presents to create dimension. The dimension is created by the placement of value and/or color. When three 60° diamonds are sewn together, they create a cube. To create dimension, consider a light source and the shadows that it creates. If the light source is coming from the upper left side of the cube, the top of the cube would be light; the right side would be in the shadows, so it would be dark; and the left side would receive a bit of light, so it would be medium.

Shading of cube

If the light source is kept consistent on all cubes, they will look stacked—almost like stairs—when sewn together.

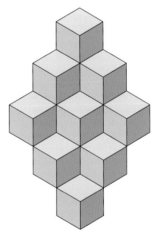

Stair-step effect when cubes are joined

As you change the direction of the light source, different sides are shaded, changing the perception of the dimension, as shown in the following four illustrations.

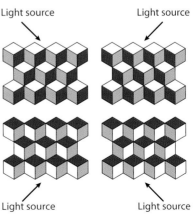

Effect of changing light source direction

CONSTRUCTING TUMBLING BLOCK UNITS

To learn to construct a tumbling block unit, you will need to choose three colors—a light, a medium, and a dark. We are considering this a sample to learn the sewing technique and not to be made into anything once it is finished, so just use scraps from previous projects. We are using white (A), black (B), and red (C) for our sample.

> *tip* We find that if you starch the fabric to be a bit stiffer than normal before cutting the strips, the diamonds are easier to control and sew. If they are limp, it is hard to keep the edges even and to start and stop exactly on the dots. Starch really helps with precision sewing.

Cut a 2½″ strip of fabric from each color. Position one strip horizontally on your cutting mat. We suggest you work with only a double thickness for precise cutting. Cutting through four layers can often cause distorted angles.

> *tip* If you are working with stripes, you will need all the strips facing up in a single thickness. If they are folded double, half the strips could end up being a mirror image of the other half and will not work in the design. Plan the direction of the stripes on paper and then align your ruler angle on the strip to accommodate the needed direction. You could also make a template of clear template plastic and draw the stripes onto it for precise placement.

Cutting stripes

Using a 3½″ ruler, align the 60° line along the top edge of the strip. This will establish the angle. Cut off the end of the strip at this angle. Rotate the strip so that the angle is now on the left. Align the 60° line of the ruler along the lower edge of the strip and measure from the end of the strip over 2½″. This will create a 60° diamond. Cut. Continue cutting the entire strip into diamonds, as well as the strips of the other two fabrics.

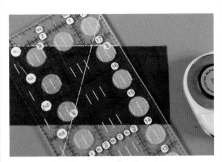

Ruler placement for first 60° cut

Ruler placement for second 60° cut

We find that using two rulers gives us the most accurate cutting. Start by placing a 60° ruler on the edge of the strip first, aligning the edge with a line on the ruler. Position the straight ruler at the 2½″ line on the cut edge and against the side of the 60° ruler. Once everything is aligned exactly, move the 60° ruler and cut against the right edge of the straight ruler.

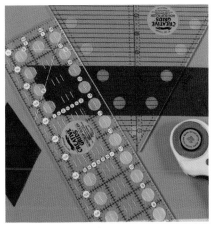

Using two rulers for most accurate cut

> *tip* If you do not know what size strip to cut, measure the pattern or diamond needed between the two parallel sides and add seam allowances.
>
> Measuring for size of diamond
>
> The fabric strips are cut this width.

Once the cutting is finished, either mark the seamlines along the cut edges of each piece or mark a dot at each intersection. This is really important, as you don't want to sew past the seam intersections when sewing the diamonds together. Using either Perfect Patchwork Templates or a template you have made yourself, mark the intersections, using the holes in the template for placement. If you prefer a line, draw the stitching line on all four sides of the diamonds. The diamonds are now ready to piece together.

Marking dots or seamlines with template—both homemade and Perfect Patchwork

Lay out the diamonds to form a cube as shown in the illustration below. We are keeping the white (A) at the top, the black (B) on the right side, and the red (C) on the left side. If you prefer to place the colors in a different arrangement, refer to the illustration about light source (page 20). Whichever way you like the color position, keep all the cubes the same. You might find that marking the letters A, B, and C on the corresponding diamonds will help you keep the orientation straight.

Layout of pieces

You will piece one seam at a time. Begin by placing a white (A) and black (B) diamond right sides together. Place a pin exactly through the dots at both ends of the seams. Check both sides to be sure they are accurate on the underneath side. (If you cut very accurately, the diamond edges will align exactly.) Place the

diamonds under the needle, white diamond up, and manually lower the needle through the first dot. Remove the pin and hold the thread tails out to the left side of the foot.

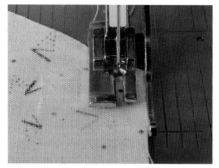

Needle position at beginning of seam

Lower the presser foot and secure the stitch.

Seam starting and stopping at dot

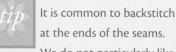

tip It is common to backstitch at the ends of the seams. We do not particularly like this, as it leaves a lump of thread at the end of each seam. If you get used to reducing the stitch length, you will find that you have much more control of the needle coming up to the dots and the stitching. A longer stitch, or backstitching, is much more likely to jump beyond the stopping point, requiring you to remove a stitch or two at the ends of some seams. Every bit of control you gain when sewing will eliminate wasted time trying to fix the problem.

note *You might find other instructions telling you to sew off one end of the seam each time you sew. This does work, but it does not allow you to fan the seams at the intersections without taking out the tiny stitches. All the seams are pressed to the side, but a lump occurs when they all come together. We would suggest that you try it both ways and see which way you prefer.*

tip Take it easy with steam and starch when pressing these pieces. You are better off starting out with more heavily starched fabric than adding starch as you go. The diamond shapes have to stay the exact same size as each other throughout the process, and if one gets distorted or the size changes at the ironing board, the problem will continue to grow, and the distortion caused by this is irreversible.

From the front side, determine the position of the third (C) diamond. Lay the red (C) diamond on top of the white (A) diamond, right sides together, and pin at the dots on both ends of the seam. Turn the unit over so that you are stitching on the white side. Stitch from dot to dot, going toward the intersection. You want to stop exactly at the previously sewn seam. Remember to shorten your stitches on both ends.

Press the seam allowance toward the white (A) diamond.

Position of third diamond

Rotate the red (C) diamond to align with the last remaining edge to be joined. Pin so that you can sew from the outer dot to the inside seam. Fold the white diamond in half so that the seam to be sewn aligns exactly. Because you are pressing all the seams in one direction, these seams will interlock (butt together), which helps you check for perfect alignment. Pin this seam in place, making sure all raw edges are aligned exactly. Check that the inner corners of the black (B) and red (C) diamonds are aligned; then pin in place. Align the piece in the machine so that you are again sewing toward the intersection. *Pull the seam allowances back and out of the way as you approach them.* Once the seam is finished, check that no seam allowance has been caught in any of the stitching.

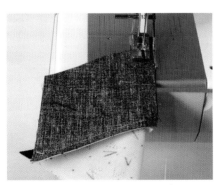
Last seam of third diamond

Press all the seam allowances in the same direction—counterclockwise. This will create a "fanned" intersection, similar to what we did for Four-Patch and Nine-Patch blocks in Volume 1, Class 150, Lesson Six (page 58).

Spinning seam allowances—back

Y-seam on front

If all went well, all three points should come together perfectly on the front of the block. If there is a hole, you didn't sew close enough to the previous line of stitching. If there is a tuck, you have sewn beyond the dot too far into the seam allowance.

The next step is to turn this one tumbling block unit into a large hexagon of three tumbling block units. This system makes it easier to build a design than working with a lot of small, individual tumbling block units.

Position another black (B) diamond on top of the left side of the white (A) diamond. Turn it over so the white diamond is on the top. Align all the edges. Stitch from dot to dot, or just up to the stitching. Press toward the black (B) diamond. If you analyze the pressing pattern that is starting to develop, it will tell you which way to press to keep the new seam going in the same direction as the previous pressing.

Black diamond added

Position another red (C) diamond on the right side of the white (A) diamond, right sides together. Pin at the dots to align the pieces exactly. Turn the unit over and sew from dot to dot again. Press toward the white (A) diamond. With this red diamond on top, align the edges of the black and red diamonds and pin in place. This is a point where you want to make sure all the diamonds are still aligning perfectly. Pin the two together and sew dot to dot. Press toward the red diamond. You will see the spin start to happen again. Fan the seams at the intersection to create a very flat unit.

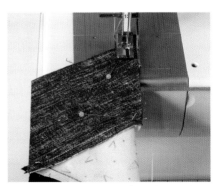
Stitching second side of red diamond

You now have half of a hexagon. Repeat the above process to create the second half.

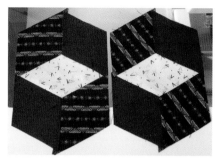

Two halves of hexagon

You are now ready to combine the two halves. Be sure to pin carefully. There are two ways to approach this seam. One way is to stitch through the center points when joining them together. Another way is to continue with the dot-to-dot system. You might want to try both, see which gives you the best results, and choose the one you like the best. Either way, pin the points of the two white (A) diamonds exactly where they meet. This is very much like matching triangles. Open the seam allowance, visually align the point, and pin. Next, abut all the seams within the entire block and pin. Because of the counterclockwise pressing, all the seams will nest together. This ensures that the block is staying accurate. If anything is out of square at this point, go back and check that all the seams are straight and accurate.

Stitching two halves together

Once everything is pinned in place, sew the seam from dot to dot—either outside dot to center dot or outside dot through the center to the opposite outside dot. Take out the pins and check to see that the points of the white (A) diamonds touch exactly. You may have to do this a couple of times to learn exactly where the perfect alignment spot is. Press the seams. If you sew through the center, open the seam allowance and press flat. If you stitch dot to dot, the seam allowances will continue to rotate counterclockwise.

Back of joined halves

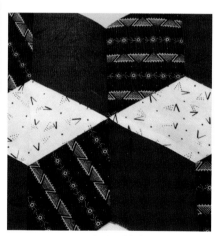

Front of joined halves

Once the two halves are joined, you will need to add the last two white (A) diamonds. Insert them into the top and bottom of the unit, following the same process as before. Press the seams to rotate counterclockwise. Press well from the front side and pat yourself on the back for your accom-

plishment. Once you get the hang of this type of piecing, it actually becomes enjoyable.

Adding final two white diamonds

These large hexagons can now be made in multiples and joined to create a larger quilt top. The following illustration shows how to join the hexagons, as well as the units needed for the corners and edges.

Layout of hexagon units

If you would rather not join multiples of tumbling block units together into larger hexagons, you can join the individual units together into rows, and then join the rows as the next illustration shows.

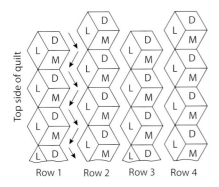

Top side of quilt

Row 1   Row 2   Row 3   Row 4

Sewing individual units together into rows and then joining rows

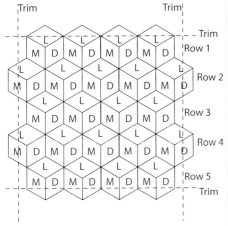

Trim   Trim

Trim
Row 1
Row 2
Row 3
Row 4
Row 5
Trim

Rows sewn together and trimmed

COLOR PLACEMENT REALLY MAKES A DIFFERENCE

Now that you know how to join the cubes (we are calling three cubes joined together a "trio"), let's change the color placement of each cube and see what we get. This time you will not add the outside diamonds that turn the three cubes into a hexagon. Instead, you will make as many cube trios as your design requires. For our example, we are making five rows of four cube trios, so we need 18 cube trios, or 54 individual tumbling block units.

Once the units are constructed, lay out three units, positioning them so that the dark side is on the outside point of each.

Layout plan for units before sewing into trios

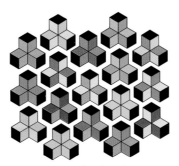

Layout plan for trios

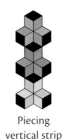

Piecing vertical strip

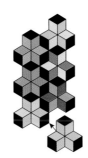

Create row to side by adding one trio of cubes at a time.

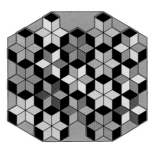

Trios sewn together

If the above design intrigues you, use your graph paper and color in the stars that are created, as well as defining the diamonds that surround the stars. Color placement and the use of a dark surrounding the colors can be a fun design challenge. Ready for more? Read on.

LESSON TWO:
Designing with 60° angles

The blocks shown here were created from a hexagon divided into various units to create interior lines that keep repeating the 60° angle. We will look at 60° diamonds and how they make wonderful stars in Class 430. However, if you take the simple 60° diamond and start to divide it in different directions within the diamond, you will be amazed at what you will start to develop. We know that you are probably having fun with this but are starting to sweat a bit about the amount of work involved in the piecing. Just keep in mind how wonderful your original design will be when made up in fabric—far more exciting and stunning than a Rail Fence!

If you divide the hexagon into three diamonds, you will get a simple Tumbling Block. Draw lines from the center to every other point of the hexagon.

Tumbling Blocks

Divide the hexagon in half from point to point. When three of these half-hexagon shapes are joined, they form an equilateral triangle.

Half-hexagon shape

Another shape is created when six of the half-hexagon units are joined. When many of this unit are combined, the design is often called Inner City.

Another fun shape

Here are a few more ideas for dividing a basic hexagon into unique shapes. Can you come up with any others? Photocopy these blocks and play with them in repeats to see what patterns emerge when they are joined.

Ten different blocks made by dividing basic hexagon

Are you wondering what to do with these blocks? Look at the following illustrations and discover what happens when other 60° units are added to the basic hexagon shape.

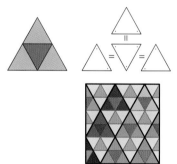

Using just 60° triangles to design—also known as Pyramids

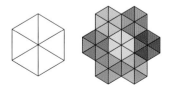

Piece six triangles together to form a hexagon, and design with hexagons side by side.

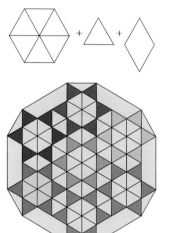

Pieced hexagons with 60° diamonds and 60° triangles

Now is a great time to get out the graph paper and colored pencils and start coloring.

What fun to be able to create your own designs so easily!

STRETCHING SQUARE BLOCKS INTO DIAMONDS

Now we will work with ordinary patchwork blocks and mirrors. This process can mess with your mind a bit, but it is fun to learn and witness the results. When a patchwork block is stretched from a square into a diamond, every unit in the block becomes a diamond or a portion of one. The best results come from blocks designed on a four-patch or nine-patch grid and include more than one shape or shape size. Look at the following blocks. Avoid blocks with diagonal seams at the corners (half-square triangles for example) to keep from having long skinny points and difficult seams to match when you join the blocks together. The most basic design to start with is the Nine-Patch. Watch what happens when it is put into a diamond.

60° Nine-Patch

Now combine three of these 60° diamonds and color in the nine-patch squares. You get a dimensional cube shape that is really a complex tumbling block unit.

Nine-patch Tumbling Block

If you place six of these nine-patch diamonds together, you get a six-pointed star, which we will discuss in detail in Class 430.

Six nine-patch diamonds make six-pointed star.

The placement of color can dramatically change the look of these diamonds. Following is a grouping of other patchwork blocks stretched into a diamond.

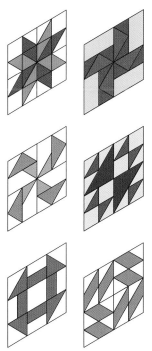

Various blocks stretched into 60° diamonds

Find other blocks that you would like to experiment with and draw them on graph paper. Once you have the diamonds drawn, use the mirrors that we introduced in Volume 3, Class 330, Lesson Five (page 41). You will see that if you put the mirrors in the top left corner of the blocks above, you get three repeats of the block, turning it into a Tumbling Block. If the mirrors are placed in the longer point, you get six repeats, making a star with six complex points.

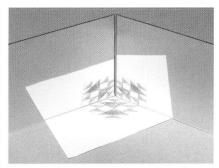

Using mirrors to see pattern repeat—corner

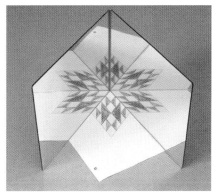

Using mirrors to see pattern repeat—point

You can also do this by making photocopies of your drawings and gluing them together to see the final effect.

Gluing multiples together

Before we leave this idea, let's go one step further. The repeats shown earlier are all repeats of the stretched block colored as the block would normally be designed. What if we play off the shapes within each diamond and change how they interconnect with each other where the edges join? We change the placement of the colors to create a totally new interplay of the shapes.

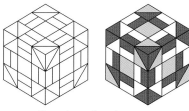

Changing color placement

We realize that the sewing of some of these designs can be a bit daunting, but the grid can be enlarged substantially and still yield the stunning effects of the dimensions created. Keep playing until you come up with something that is truly worth the time it takes to piece.

LESSON THREE:
The quilts

Let's back up and calm things down a bit. If you are like us, you can get overstimulated by the multitude of ideas your brain can come up with. Just using the basic tools of graph paper and colored pencils, you can create more ideas than you could ever have time to sew! Start a file of ideas you like for later consideration.

For the first project, we are going to make simple tumbling block units using paper foundations and appliqué them onto a background. The individual Tumbling Blocks can be made out of any fabric, including cute baby prints, small panel prints cut to size, or fussy-cut alphabet letters to be placed on each side of the Tumbling Block. Have fun with this easy project.

PROJECT ONE: *TUMBLING BLOCK BABY QUILT*

Tumbling Block Baby Quilt

Stitching order to create Tumbling Blocks

Quilt top size: 51″ × 61″

Block size: 8½″ finished

Diamond size: 3″ six-point diamonds

Diamonds needed: 60

Yardages needed:

   1⅝ yards white

   ⅛ yard each of 36 different fabrics in
   12 different 3-color combinations

   ⅓ yard dark blue solid

   1¾ yards fabric for border*

** You will only need ¾ yard of border fabric
if you choose to use a fabric that is not directional and can easily be pieced to create the
border lengths needed.*

For this fun baby quilt, Carrie chose
to work with 3″ precut six-point
diamond papers from Paper Pieces.
Start by straightening your fabric
and then cutting the fabric into 3½″-
wide strips. This way you will get
eight rectangles per strip. To cut the
individual diamonds easily, precut
each strip into 3½″ × 5″ rectangles.

Next, just as you did for the hexagon
project using the paper pieces, trim
your fabric rectangles to extend ³⁄₁₆″
beyond the paper for seam allowances.
Turn the edge and glue the fabric over
the edge, making sure that you have a
crisp, sharp edge.

Set up your machine for the gathering
stitch (page 13). Use invisible nylon,
100/2 silk, or 60/2 machine embroidery thread on top. The thread needs
to match the different color combinations of your Tumbling Blocks.

Lay out all 20 of your Tumbling
Blocks, positioning the diamonds the
way you want them to look once they
are sewn. Pick up the two bottom diamonds of the first combination and
stitch them together corner to corner.
Add the top diamond, stitching the
two sides to create your first completed Tumbling Block.

Repeat this for the remaining 19
individual Tumbling Blocks.

Once your Tumbling Blocks are
made, it is time to appliqué them
to your background squares. Cut
20 squares, 10½″ square.

Fold each of the background squares
in half and lightly press. Fold a
second time in the opposite direction and press again. This divides
the square evenly and gives you the
center point.

Pressing lines for background fabric

Place one Tumbling Block on the
background square, aligning it with
the pressing lines. Where all three
diamonds of the block meet is the
point that needs to align exactly with
the center intersection of your background block. Using a small spot of
glue from your gluestick, or appliqué
pins, temporarily secure the block in
place. You are now ready to appliqué
the block onto the background.

We are including a short explana-
tion of how to appliqué the blocks
using the machine. In case you are
interested in exploring machine
appliqué further, Harriet has written
a book—a technical workbook for all
forms of machine appliqué, *Mastering
Machine Appliqué*—that will tell
you all the details of how to create
professional-looking appliqué on the
machine. Here is a brief set of instructions to get you started.

Set up your machine with a size 60/8 needle, 60-weight two-ply fine cotton machine embroidery thread in the bobbin (Mettler with green printing on the spool), clear nylon in the top, and an open-toe embroidery foot on the machine.

Supplies needed to appliqué centers

The stitch used is a very tiny blind stitch. If your machine won't allow you to make a blind stitch that is very narrow and very short, use a blanket stitch. The distance between the zigzags should be no more than ⅛". A little bit shorter is actually better. If your machine changes width in increments of 0.5, try to stitch with a 0.5 width. If this is too narrow to hit the edge, go up to the next number, keeping it as narrow as possible. Make sure the stitch bites into the very edge of the tumbling block unit. You are trying to make the stitch totally invisible on the top.

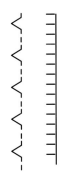

Stitches used for invisible appliqué

Do a test sample before starting on the Tumbling Blocks. Bring the bobbin thread up to the top, positioning the needle so that it goes into the background fabric as close to the edge of the block as possible. When the machine makes the straight stitches, they should be in the background fabric, with the needle rubbing the edge of the block. When the needle swings over to the left to make the zigzag, it should just enter at the very edge of the block, catching no more than two threads in from the edge of the Tumbling Block. Stitch slowly and keep the needle rubbing the edge.

If you see bobbin thread come up into the needle holes, reduce the top tension and/or tighten the bobbin tension until you no longer see the bobbin thread. Appliqué around the six sides of the block. Continue with the remaining 19 Tumbling Blocks.

Appliquéing around Tumbling Block

Now that all your blocks are appliquéd, remove the background fabric under the block and then remove the papers from the diamonds, as you did with the placemats in Class 410 (page 16). Once this is completed, set your iron on the wool temperature setting. Press the background square to remove the original press lines and to make sure the seam allowances are lying flat. When all 20 blocks are pressed, measure and trim each of the blocks.

Using a 9½" square ruler, place the vertical 4½" line on the vertical

intersection of the bottom two diamonds and the 4½" horizontal line on the center of the Tumbling Block and the two top diamond points. Trim the side and the top of the block along the edge of the ruler. Turn the block 180°, realign the same points, and trim the remaining two sides. You will have an exact 9" square.

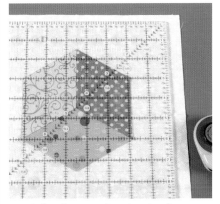

Ruler alignment for trimming down background squares

To create the sashing for this quilt, you can either use a single fabric around each block or mix them up and use all three fabrics of the corresponding Tumbling Block for that block's sashing, as Carrie did. For each block, cut four strips 1⅜" wide and 9" long. You also need to cut 30 – 2" squares of the dark blue solid for the cornerstones, as well as 18 – 1⅜" × 9" strips for the outer border.

Lay out your blocks and determine the color placement of your Tumbling Blocks. Once the blocks are in place, position the sashing strips accordingly. Place the dark solid blue strips around the outer edge of the blocks and then the cornerstones.

Time to sew again. Start by constructing the first row of sashing. Sew the four strip pairs together (one blue solid and one color that matches the block below it). Press the seam allowance to the blue solid, starch, and then trim each strip to 1″. Add the cornerstones between each strip pair and press the seam allowance to the cornerstone. Repeat this with each of the sashing rows.

Sashing row

Next, sew together the strip pairs that are between the blocks. Press and trim them to 1″. Sew the strips onto the blocks and then sew the entire row together. Press the seam allowances toward the blocks.

Block row

Once all the rows are constructed, you can sew them together.

The last step is to put the outer border on the quilt. As noted in the fabric yardage section, because Carrie chose to use a directional print, she needed to cut two strips on lengthwise grain 5½″ wide by 52″ long. Refer back to Volume 1, Class 180 (page 95) on measuring borders.

Cut the top and bottom border on the crosswise grain 5½″ wide by 42″. Then cut four cornerstones 5½″ square and add them to the ends of the top and bottom border.

And that's it … this is a great quilt to make for a toddler or young child. You could use a wide variety of themed fabrics and make it a really fun *I Spy* quilt! Get creative and have fun!

PROJECT TWO: *BLUE STAIRS TO HEAVEN*

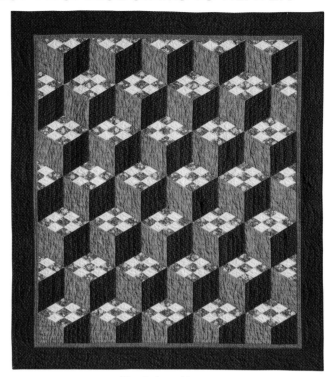
Blue Stairs to Heaven

Quilt top size: 45″ × 50″

Block size: 4½″ finished (flat side to flat side)

Diamond size: cut 5″

Yardages needed:

¾ yard cream

⅞ yard blue print

1⅛ yards medium blue tonal

1⅛ yards dark blue print

This great throw quilt is not only fun to make but also will delight anyone who sees it with its great dimensional design. You can change the look of each block by substituting any pieced block for the Nine-Patch as discussed in Lesson Two (page 26). Use a variety of blocks and mix them up for a really dynamic affect.

To start, cut 15 strips 2″ wide of the blue print fabric and 12 strips 2″ wide of the cream fabric.

From these strips, create nine-patch strip sets, sewing six sets of dark-light-dark and three sets of light-dark-light. Press the seam allowances in the direction of the arrows on the illustration.

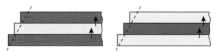
Strip sets needed—offset ends

Offset each strip on the left end of each strip set by about 2″ from the previous strip sewn. This will give a little extra fabric in which you can squeeze out an extra segment if needed.

Using a 60° triangle ruler, align the horizontal lines of the ruler with the seamlines of your strip set. Place a 2½″ or 3½″ × 12″ ruler alongside the 60° triangle ruler. Make sure the 60° line of the straight ruler is aligned with the bottom edge of the strip set. Slide the triangle ruler over a bit and make your first cut. This establishes the 60° angle. Turn the strip 180° and place the 2″ line of the straight ruler on the cut edge of the strip set. Position the triangle ruler alongside the straight ruler, keeping the horizontal lines on the seamlines. Once you have double-checked all the angles and measurements, move the triangle ruler and cut a segment. Continue this process until you have cut all the segments. Refer to Lesson One (page 21) for instructions on using two rulers to ensure that the 60° angle stays accurate.

You will need to cut a total of 76 segments of the dark-light-dark strip sets (A) and 38 segments of the light-dark-light strip sets (B).

Each diamond is made up of two A segments and one B segment. There are two critical places that the seamlines need to match when sewing these segments together. Place a light-dark-light segment (A) on top of a dark-light-dark segment (B). Offset the segments so that the ends form a V. The "crotch" of the V is where the needle must enter and exit when sewing the seam. If the segments are not aligned prop-erly, the strip seams will not align within the seam, and the edges will not be straight when pressed.

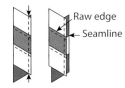

V and seam alignment close-up

Align the first seam allowances before you start to sew. To make a perfect intersecting match of the two seg-ments, match the raw edge of the top

segment seam allowance with the underneath seamline. Hold or pin in place. Make sure you either hold your threads tight when you start to sew or use a scrap of fabric to start with. Stitch through the first seam and continue sewing to the next seam.

Raw edge exactly on underneath seam

Repeat with the second seam.

Second seam match

As you come to the end, be sure that the ends are aligned so that the V is formed and the needle exits exactly in the V.

Sewing through V

Chainstitch all 38 pairs together in the same manner. Press the seams open.

Align the third segment, making sure that the seam allowances are facing the foot of the machine. With the larger unit on the bottom, add the third segment to the top. A slick way to get the V at the beginning just right is to match the first intersecting

seam when aligning the raw edges of the two units. Once this seam is positioned, the V automatically forms correctly. Press seams open again.

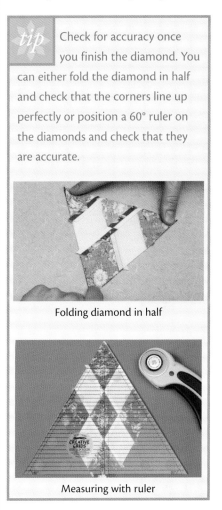

tip Check for accuracy once you finish the diamond. You can either fold the diamond in half and check that the corners line up perfectly or position a 60° ruler on the diamonds and check that they are accurate.

Folding diamond in half

Measuring with ruler

Next, cut the solid diamonds from the two other fabrics. Straighten your fabrics and cut seven 5″ strips of each fabric. Cut 35 – 5″-wide diamonds from each of the fabrics, again using the 60° triangle ruler and a 6″-wide straight ruler together for accuracy.

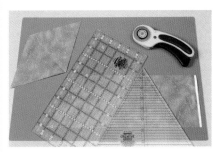

Ruler alignment for cutting solid diamonds

Once all the diamonds are cut and the nine-patch diamonds are constructed, mark the four dots in the corners for alignment. Use a 60° diamond template (make your own or use a Perfect Patchwork template) for easy marking, using the holes in the templates. You can also use the template to trim the long points off the diamonds if you choose—it will make sewing a little easier.

Lay out your diamonds in the formation you have chosen for your quilt. Pick up a diamond of any color and position it, right sides together, on a diamond of a second color. Line up the dots and sew from dot to dot, just as you did with the sample tumbling block unit (page 22). Repeat this with all the diamonds of the same two colors. Do not press when you are finished. Once you have the third diamond attached, the seams will be pressed so that they lie flat and the intersection fans.

Now add the third diamond—sew one seam first for all 32 blocks and then sew the second seam.

Sewing order for diamonds

Now it is time to press. The seams will rotate in either a clockwise or a counterclockwise fashion, creating a fanned center where the seams intersect. You will also need to create six half-blocks—three with just a dark diamond on the right and three with just a light diamond on the left.

Quilt construction time! It is easiest to sew this quilt together in rows.

Start by sewing five of the blocks side by side. You will need four rows with five blocks each. There will be three alternate rows with four blocks each and two half-blocks at each end (see photo on page 30 for placement). Make sure that you nest the seam allowances of the two blocks where they meet to ensure that the points of your diamonds line up properly.

Next, sew hexagon to hexagon as you did for the *Mosaic Star* (page 18). This will be easier than before, as the hexagons are much larger. Line up the sides of the two hexagons to be sewn, align the dots, and make sure that the seams are nested together. Sew from dot to dot. Remove the blocks from under the machine and realign the sides that are to be stitched next. Line up the dots and the seam allowances and sew from dot to dot. Keep repeating this process until the rows are all sewn together.

Once this is done, trim up the edges. Line up a long ruler with the nine-patch diamonds at the top of the quilt. Measure ⅜″ to the right of the middle row of small diamonds and trim away the extra fabric.

Trimming top of quilt

The sides also need to be cut so that they are even with the raw edge of the last block of the rows of five blocks. You will be trimming away half of the pieced diamonds of the half-blocks.

Add borders if you choose. Carrie chose to add a narrow ½″ border of pink for a little sparkle on the quilt top and then a 5″ border of the dark blue.

PROJECT THREE: *CONSTELLATION*

Constellation

Quilt size:
26″ × 37″

Constellation is going to be your first "exam." As this is your senior year in quilting, at this point, you should have a good grasp of the techniques and skills we are teaching you, and you should be able to translate those skills to any project.

If you have done all or even just a couple of the projects in Class 410 and this class, then you should see that this quilt is no more difficult than what you have done previously with hexagons. In *Constellation,* you will be cutting diamonds to make up hexagons and then setting the hexagons together in rows.

Carrie used template #44 from Set G of Marti Michell's Perfect Patchwork Templates to cut her diamonds.

Look at the following illustration and count the number of blue hexagons and the number of hexagons with yellow that you will need.

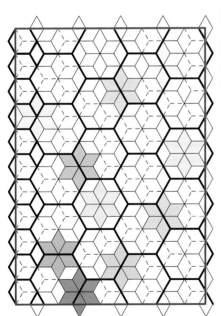

Hexagon breakout with star placement

Did you get 63 all-blue hexagons and 33 hexagons with yellow for the stars? If not, go back and count again to make sure you know where the number came from. Take the number of hexagons and multiply that by three, as there are three diamonds needed to make up each hexagon.

You should come up with 288. Now count the number of single diamonds you need. Do you get 26? How many of the total number need to be yellow diamonds? 66? You are on your way to figuring your yardage.

Now it's time to pick your fabrics. In Carrie's case, she used 17 blues variegated from very light to very dark and 11 different yellows shaded from light to dark. Do you have that many fabrics, or fewer?

To determine the yardage you will need, you need to know how many hexagons you need from each fabric. If you, like Carrie, have 17 blues, divide the total number of blue diamonds needed by the number of blue fabrics you have. If you need 314 diamonds total and 66 of those are yellow, you need a total of 248 blue diamonds; that divided by 17 gives you 14.5, or 15 diamonds from each fabric. Now determine how many diamonds you can get from a strip of fabric. With the template Carrie used, the template edge that aligns with the straight grain is 2⅝″. Divide 42″ by 2.625″, and you get 16, which is one more than needed. Carrie was able to purchase just ⅛-yard pieces of all of her fabric because she only needed a single 2⅝″ strip of each. What will you need with the number of fabrics you have chosen and the size template you have picked?

Once your yardage is figured, it's time to get your diamonds cut out and then laid out. Use the following illustration to help you with color placement.

Color placement layout for *Constellation*

And that's it. The rest is up to you! You have enough experience now to determine how you want to sew this quilt together and what will give you the best results.

Good luck!

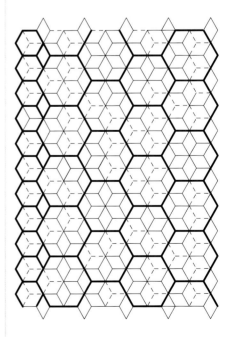

Class 430

A gallery of six-pointed stars

This class is going to take 60°diamonds, as well as equilateral triangles, and make them into multipiece units that then become more elaborate six-pointed stars. Stars made with 60° diamonds come in many configurations. We have included several of our favorites for you to play with. We suggest that you study the dissection of each of the first set of stars and try your hand at drafting them.

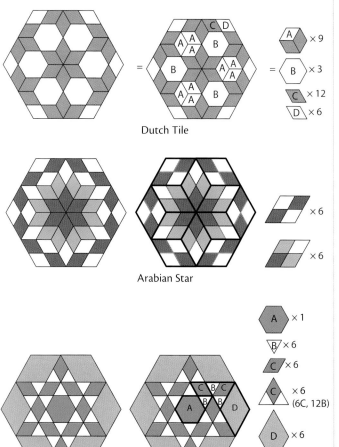

Dutch Tile

Arabian Star

Ozark Diamonds

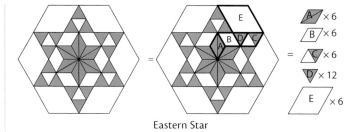

Eastern Star

You will find that several of the stars in the following group look very complicated. As you are drafting and/or dissecting them, keep in mind the size of diamonds you like to work with and how big the star will become with that size diamond. When a diamond has a seam down the center, can you utilize a striped fabric to eliminate a seam and make the piecing easier? Would it be easier to work over paper, as you learned in Class 410 (page 13), if the pieces are small? You are gaining skills that will allow you to make these decisions as you design your own quilts.

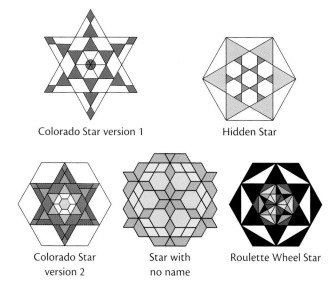

Colorado Star version 1

Hidden Star

Colorado Star version 2

Star with no name

Roulette Wheel Star

LESSON TWO:

Designing with 60° diamonds

Books documenting antique quilts document hundreds of quilts that were made using 60° diamonds. Many of them use all three elements of the 60° angle—hexagons, diamonds, and triangles. You are gaining the skills that will enable you to adapt or change any antique quilt that you like.

Another fun process is to try to reinterpret a pattern that is a different angle into a 60° angle. Can you change an eight-pointed star into a 60° angle? Working on equilateral triangle graph paper is a requirement when working through changing or developing patterns with angles. Often the new pattern doesn't resemble the original at all.

TRIANGLES

We can't overlook the equilateral triangles that are left over from cutting diamonds, or designing with these triangles. When you cut them from stripes or strata, you can make even more movement appear. Patterns that work with both diamonds and triangles give us good opportunities to play with incorporating stripes into the design.

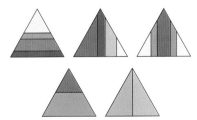

Cutting triangles from stripes or strata

Stripes can add so much detail and eliminate a lot of sewing. If you cannot find a stripe that suits your design, you can create one by sewing

strips together—called strata. By playing with different widths and angles, you can achieve a very detailed-looking unit using simple pieces.

Because the triangles are equilateral, they can be turned two or three different ways in the pattern. Here are some examples of playing with stripes and the effect they give to a hexagon. You can see that if the stripes are too symmetrical, there is less variety in the placement. The more stripes and the more varied the size, the more potential for playing.

TRIANGLES WITH STRIPES IN HEXAGON FORMATIONS

Another fun way to work is to cut patches from fabric and just start placing them on your design wall. Because the diamonds are all cut from the same template, there are no fitting issues. Just play with the colors and the shapes that emerge as you move the pieces around. You might call this designing or just playing. We think designing is really just playing.

STARS

Three original blocks

Another fun way to design is to combine different configurations of 60° stars. Just looking at the stars is exciting enough, but what happens when they are put together into a quilt top?

We have taken three simple star patterns and mixed them up in the following quilt top design. Each star becomes a hexagon, and by changing values and shades within each star, a soft, random pattern is developed. We have colored in one and left one empty for you to try your hand at developing the design. When coloring, don't forget that the stars do not have to be static. The colors can blend from one to the other, which would soften the lines even more

CLASS 430   35

and make the hexagon shapes less apparent. Don't forget to make good use of light, medium, and dark units. Enlarge and photocopy the line drawing several times and try different ideas. If you come up with something you really are jazzed about and think you want to construct, color-copy your design and cut out the hexagons. This would be a color legend for planning the fabric placement for each star. We hope you have fun with this exercise.

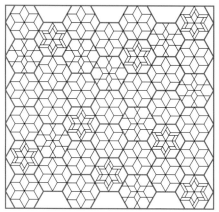

Line drawing of blocks mixed up in layout

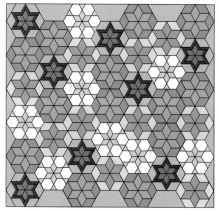

Our color version of quilt top

Basic construction technique

Now that you have had a chance to see just how exciting and complex the 60° angle can be, let's learn to construct the stars. We are going to start with a simple star of just diamonds, and then move on to a star that has nine-patch points.

The most basic 60° star is six diamonds sewn together, surrounded by six more diamonds. We are starting here so that we can get the six diamonds to meet exactly at the center. The center is the most difficult area to get accurate, as there is a lot of bulk from seam allowances to work with in a very tight space. Once you master this problem area, you will derive the benefits throughout the rest of the book.

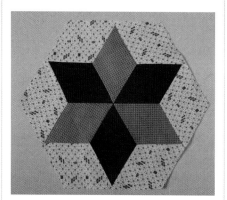

Basic 60° star

We are going to sound like a broken record by the end of the book, but you must start by being very accurate with your cutting when working with angles and set-in piecing. You can make this star from any size 60° diamonds you want. The size of the diamond is dependent on the size of the block you need. Draft your own diamond or work with templates if you have them. We are working with Set H of Perfect Patchwork Templates, diamond #52, for this block. If you want to rotary cut, cut a 3″ strip and cut 3″ – 60° diamonds.

Cut three diamonds each of two different colors and six diamonds of background fabric. Mark the seamline dots in each corner and point of each piece. Begin by sewing the star points into pairs. Start the stitching at the dot in the corner and sew off the edge at the points of these three pairs. Press toward the darker diamonds.

Sewing points into pairs

When joining the points, you will find that the seam allowances of the first two pairs butt together. Make the entire length of the seam butt snugly. Place a couple of the finest pins you have (we love the extra-fine Clover Patchwork Pins) right in the stitching of the seam. Align all the raw edges and pin in place. Start the seam at the outside corner again, but as you approach the point, stop and pull back the underneath seam allowance so that it does not get caught in the stitching. If you have placed a pin in the previous stitching, it will help keep the butted seam from slipping as you pull the underneath seam allowance out of the way. Stitch to the seam, stopping exactly at the previous stitching line.

When you open the unit to the right side, check to see that the seam remained butted and the two points are exactly aligned. If this did not happen, take out the stitching and try again. Do not press this seam, as it is easier to manipulate the seam allowances at the point if they are not pressed flat.

The third unit is the trickiest to add. This time push a very fine pin into the seam of the third unit, right at the dot for the point. Next, position the third unit on the first two and butt one of the seams. Push the pin just into the intersection of the two points, hold tight, and swing the pin to take the pin stitch in the butted seam. This should hold the points in alignment and prevent slippage as you stitch. Stitch from the outside corner to the pin. When you open the units to the front, check that five points are now aligned exactly. Repeat this process for the last seam.

If everything went well, all six points will meet in the center. If they are off just a thread and it is not noticeable, leave it alone. If it is obvious that the points are off, keep working at the process until you find the trick you need to keep accurate.

Press so that all the seams are spinning in the same direction and the center seam allowances are fanned.

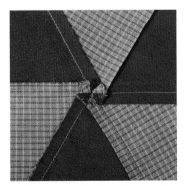

Seam allowances spinning and center fanned

Points meeting in center on front

Finish your block by adding the six background diamonds using the same method you learned when making Tumbling Blocks in Class 420 (page 21).

Back of completed block

Well done! Now let's try something a little more complex. Adding pieced units to each diamond point adds a lot of interest to this block. We are going to make each diamond into a 60° nine-patch unit. If you made *Blue Stairs to Heaven* (page 30), you have already worked through these instructions. If you didn't make that quilt, start here to make the nine-patch units. We will share some great tricks that help you make the internal seams match easily when there is a four-patch or nine-patch within the diamond unit. This will take us back to strip piecing, as the diamonds within the diamond are created by sewing three strips together and then cutting the strips into 60° segments that are sewn into a nine-patch to create the large diamond shape.

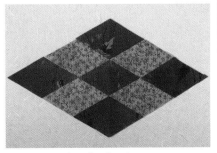

Pieced points in star

Let's get started. You will need three colors for the sample.

Cut:

> 3 – 2″ × 45″ strips from each of the two fabrics used in the star points (We used green and tan.)

> 6 – 5″-wide strips of background fabric for the outside diamonds

Start the construction of two strip sets by sewing one green and one tan strip together twice. Press toward the green and starch lightly. Check with your 2½″ ruler that both strips are exactly 1¾″ wide. Trim if necessary. Add a green strip to the tan side of one strip set and a tan strip to the green side of the second strip set. Press this seam in the same direction as the first and check the width with your ruler. Trim if necessary. Accuracy is crucial for these stars to align easily and accurately.

note Unlike with nine-patch strip sets, we are not going to press the strips onto the same color each time. We prefer to press the seams all in one direction. The direction is determined by the last round or the farthest outside diamond of each star point. If many strips are sewn together, each one is referred to as a round. If there are five strips sewn together, the one that is the farthest from the star center is Round 5, and all seam allowances will be pressed toward that strip. In this block, there are three strips, and the green diamond is the center as well as the outside point. Press all seam allowances in one direction. See the illustration and follow the arrows for direction.

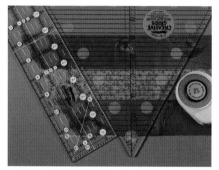

Strip sets with offset ends

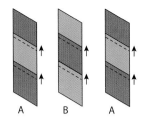

Segments that make up star points

V formed when aligning segments

Align the 60° lines of the tool of your choice (rotary ruler, Easy Six ruler, or 60° triangle) along the bottom edge and the seams of the green-tan-green strip set (A). Start at the left end if you are right-handed or the right end if you are left-handed.

Position of ruler to obtain 60° angle

Make the first cut to establish the angle. Use a 2½" ruler and measure down the strip set 2", keeping the 60° ruler lined up with the seamlines to the right of the rotary ruler. Check that all the ruler lines are in the correct position and then move the triangle ruler away with your rotary cutter. Cut the first segment along the right side of the ruler.

Continue cutting segments until you have 12. Repeat the process with the tan-green-tan strip set (B) and cut 6 segments.

Lay the segments in order beside your machine. Make sure that the seam allowances are at the top of each seam. This will have them leading in with the raw edge of the seam allowance first, making the matching process very simple.

Each star point is made up of two A segments and one B segment. There are two critical places that the seamlines need to match when sewing these segments together. The first is the V that forms at the top and bottom of the segments. The bottom segment extends and the top segment crosses over the bottom. The inside point of the V is where the needle must enter and exit when sewing the seam. If these are not aligned properly, the strip seams will not align within the seam, and the edges will not be straight when pressed.

Make sure you either hold your threads tight when you start to sew or use a scrap of fabric to start with. Sew just a few stitches and stop. You don't have far to go before you have a seam that needs to be matched. You shouldn't need pins for positioning.

Notice that the first seam you reach has been pressed to the tan and the raw edge is first to go into the machine. To make a perfect intersecting match of the two segments, match the raw edge of the top segment seam allowance with the underneath seamline. Hold in place and continue sewing to the next seam. Repeat with the second seam.

Seam on underneath raw edge

Second seam match

As you come to the end, be sure that the ends are aligned so that the V is formed and the needle exits exactly in the V.

Sewing through V

Chainstitch all six pairs together in the same manner. Press the seams open. Check the width of the sewn units after pressing to retain your accuracy.

Align the third segment, making sure that the seam allowances are facing the foot of the machine. With the larger unit on the bottom, add the third segment to the top. A slick way to get the V at the beginning just right is to match the first intersecting seam when aligning the raw edges of the two units. Once this seam is positioned, the V automatically forms correctly. Press seams open again.

 tip Check for accuracy once you finish the star point. You can either fold the point in half and check that the corners line up perfectly or position a 60° ruler on it and check that they are accurate, as illustrated in Class 420, *Blue Stairs to Heaven* (page 31).

Once the points are constructed and checked, it is time to sew them together. You will repeat the process used for the basic star, except now you have internal seams to match as well as the center point.

Start by aligning two points with right sides together, keeping all four raw edges even. The seams that have to intersect are pressed differently. The one on top is pressed open, and the

lower one is pressed to the side. To align these for a perfect match, insert a very fine pin exactly into the seam of the top unit. Push it through and guide it to come out exactly on the stitching (the thread) of the lower unit. Take the pin stitch and have the pin follow along both seams. When you look at the back, the pin is right on top of the thread the entire length. When you look at the top, the pin is in the "ditch" of the seam. Pin both intersecting seams in this manner. Start the stitching at the point and stitch from the raw edge of the point to the seamline dot at the outer edge. Repeat this process to make three pairs.

Inserting pin into seamline

 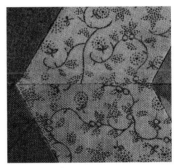
Matched seams and points on front

Sewing the three units together is a repeat of the process you did for the first sample star (page 36). The center is aligned the same, but now you also have the interior seams to align. Sew two pairs together and then add the third. Press these seams open.

Once the star is constructed, add the outside diamonds to finish the block.

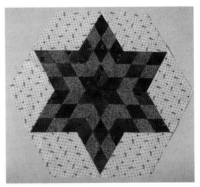
Finished block

This block can be used to design quilts that look very much like Lone Stars. Depending on color placement, you can get a lot of design impact by using only two colors or up to nine different ones. It is all in the placement of the colors. If you enjoyed making this star, play around with different colors and prints to see what you can come up with. This star is actually one of the easiest in this course.

Row 1
Row 2
Row 3

Two colors in star

Row 1
Row 2
Row 3

Five colors in star

Row 1
Row 2
Row 3
Row 4
Row 5

Center

Nine colors in star

You are now ready to start to build a quilt using 60° stars. These quilts will really show off your new skills!

LESSON FOUR:
The quilts

PROJECT ONE: *FRENCH BOUTONNIÈRE*

French Boutonnière

Quilt size: 50″ × 53″ (without borders)

Yardages needed:

Star points—up to 4 yards, depending on the spacing of the print if you are fussy cutting

½ yard pink solid

Yellow fat quarter

1⅝ yards green

We chose this quilt to start with as it utilizes fussy cutting and there are slightly fewer points to contend with than in the next quilt. Also, the pieces are fairly large. Begin this project by making your own templates using the shapes on page 41 as a guide. The accuracy of your templates will totally dictate the accuracy of the piecing, so make them very carefully out of a template material that will stand up to the rotary cutter blade when cutting around the shapes. We prefer EZ Extra Thick Template Plastic. You can also draw around the templates, use a ruler to cut the fabric on the drawn line, and then double-check the cutting accuracy by aligning the template on top of the cut unit.

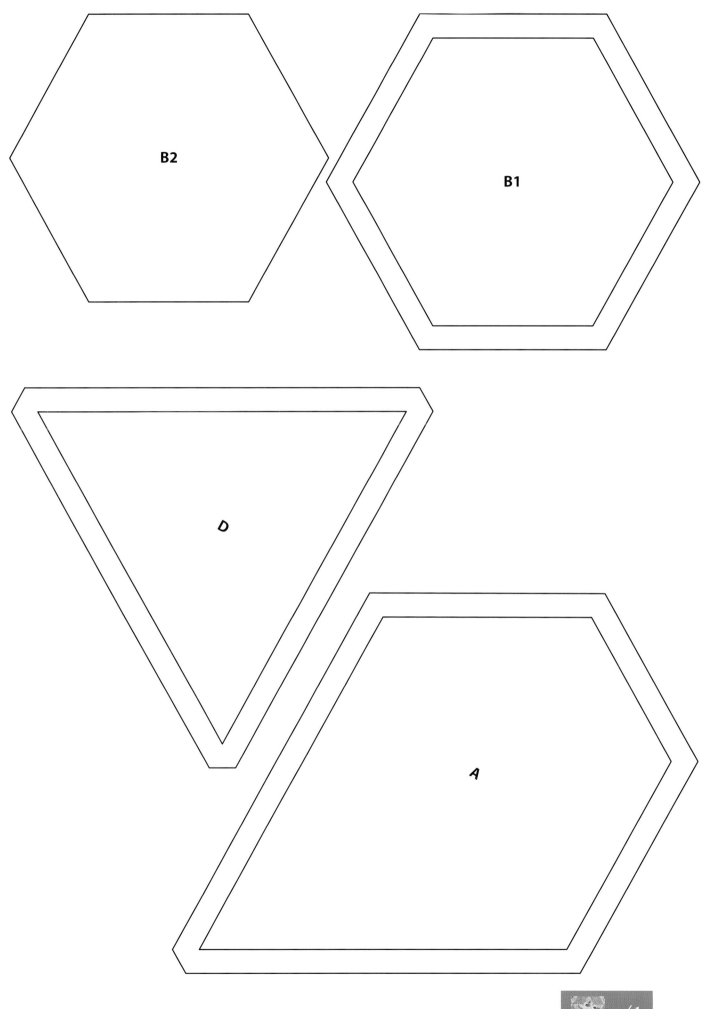

B2

B1

D

A

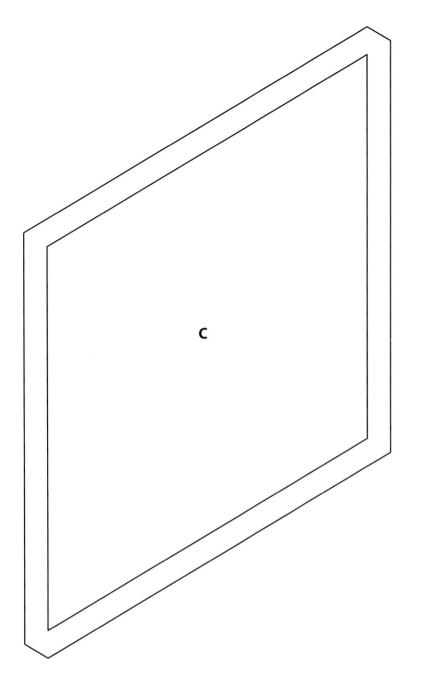

C

We chose a fabric that we could fussy cut with our template to make the star points. We lightly sketched the shape of the flower onto the top of the template to allow for accurate placement of the template on the fabric for each cut.

Fussy cutting star points

Our fabric had two different flowers that could be cut within the size of our template. Fussy cutting like this does waste a lot of fabric, so when choosing a fabric for this use, be sure to buy plenty. We appliquéd the center hexagon instead of piecing it in, but you can choose to do either.

Cut:

108 fussy-cut flowers of template A

18 yellow hexagons of template B1 or B2

71 green diamonds of template C

14 background diamonds of template D

> *tip* If you want this quilt to be larger, adding another star to the width and two more rows to the length would give you an 82″ × 97″ quilt. You would then need 32 stars. We kept the quilt smaller to entice you to try your hand at it.

Once all fabric shapes are cut, carefully mark all the dots at the seam intersections for stitching guidance on all pieces.

Begin by constructing the stars. Join the A's by sewing the side seams. Start at the blunt end, taking tiny stitches to begin. You do not have to start at the dot at this end of the seam if you are going to appliqué the center hexagon onto the completed star points. If you are going to piece it in, however, begin the stitching at the dot. Carefully align the edges of two points and stitch to the dot. Continue sewing pairs together for all the stars. Press the seams to one side. Join two pairs together next, pressing carefully after they are joined and directing the seam allowance in the same direction as the first set of seams. Add the final section, joining one seam and pressing; then close the star with the final seam. Once all the seams are joined and pressed, the star should lie perfectly flat. If it doesn't, it is a sure sign that the pieces were cut inaccurately or the seam alignment is off somewhere. Go back and double-check both and correct. If the star doesn't lie flat at this point, it will only get worse.

Star point layout

Once all 18 stars are constructed, it is time to add the centers. We chose to appliqué the centers, as it is a bit faster and gives the center a much better chance of lying flat. Prepare the centers by cutting 18 freezer paper hexagons. We have included a template (page 41) to trace for this shape without seam allowances. Trace and cut very accurately. Press the freezer paper onto the wrong side of the center fabric, leaving ½" between all the pieces. Cut a ³⁄₁₆" seam allowance beyond all edges of the freezer paper. Glue the edges over the freezer paper edge, working with a water-soluble gluestick. Be careful not to bend the paper.

We will be appliquéing the centers onto the star points, using the instructions for appliqué given in Class 420, Lesson Three (page 29).

Position the centers onto the star points, matching the points of the center hexagon with the seams of the

star point. Using a small amount of glue, glue them in place.

Do a test sample before starting on the stars. Bring the bobbin thread up to the top, positioning the needle so that it goes into the star fabric as close to the center as possible. When the machine makes the straight stitches, they should be in the star fabric, with the needle rubbing the edge of the center unit. When the needle swings over to the left to make the zigzag, it should just enter at the very edge of the center, catching no more than two threads of the center. Stitch slowly and keep the needle rubbing the edge.

If you see bobbin thread come up into the needle holes, reduce the top tension and/or tighten the bobbin tension until you no longer see the bobbin thread. Appliqué around the six sides of each center. Complete all 18 stars.

Appliquéing around center

Referring to the following illustrations, you will see that the stars now need the green diamonds added to them to get them ready to join into rows. The stars are not all the same when you do this: Six will need diamonds on all six sides, three will need diamonds on five sides, three will have two diamonds added to the top and bottom, and the inside rows have just the three stars joined with one diamond in between each pair.

Harriet found that if she sewed dot to dot on all of the diamond seams, there was too much movement and bulk in the intersection when trying to join the rows. Instead of sewing everything dot to dot, she started by sewing in every other diamond raw edge to raw edge. When inserting the alternating diamonds, she sewed dot to dot. The pressing was slightly affected by this and not as neat and tidy as usual, but the points on the top of the quilt top were excellent and well worth a bit of messy pressing on the back.

When pressing the seams as the diamonds are added, keep them spinning in the same direction so that the seams fan almost all the time.

Once the blocks are pressed, it is time to place all the units on your design wall and create rows using the following combinations:

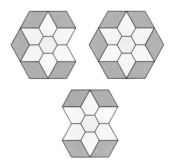

Elements for Rows 1, 3, and 5

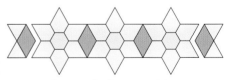

Elements for Rows 2 and 4

Once the rows are in place, you will be sewing them together in the following configuration:

Row construction plan

To cut the side wedges, you need four pieces of background fabric cut 6½″ × 23½″. Fold each piece in half vertically as shown in the diagram. Using the measurements shown, cut one 6½″ × 23½″ wedge on the folded edge of each piece. Once the fabric is folded in half, place your 60° triangle ruler on the fold to establish the cutting line. Butt a longer ruler up against the triangle to extend the straight edge. Cut the angle.

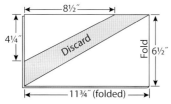

Cutting side and corner triangles

Use the remaining corner for two 8½″ × 4¼″ triangles. These are the corner units; you need a total of four.

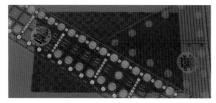

Ruler placement for cutting wedges

Begin by constructing Row 1. Set the diamond of the second star into the open space of the first star, sewing dot to dot. Once the seam is pressed, insert the triangle on the top edge, making sure the straight grain is on the outside edge. Stitch these seams off the edge instead of to the dot. Repeat this process until all the stars are joined into a row. Repeat for Rows 3 and 5.

The interior rows are stars with only one diamond between them. Join a green diamond with two background triangles as shown. Add to the end of each row.

When sewing the rows together, take your time, pin a lot, and sew carefully. Make sure all the seam allowances are pulled back out of the way when sewing all the points. If you have half of the points sewn down beyond the dot, the intersections will be easier to work with. All six points are coming together, and it can be very bulky and messy if all the seams are sewn dot to dot. You may need to experiment with one or two intersections to see what works best for you.

Start by inserting the point of the first star of Row 2 into the opening of the green diamonds of Row 1. Once the point is inserted, stitch the seam to the left of the point. Sew off the edge instead of stopping at the dot on the outside edge. Insert the second point into the diamonds of Row 1. Close the seam to the left again. Repeat this process until both rows are joined. Check your points and make sure they are very sharp and accurate on the right side of the quilt top.

Join Rows 3 and 4 and then add them onto the first two rows. Row 5 has triangles that need to be inserted on the outside edge before the row is added to the other four.

It will take a couple of hours or more to join the rows. Don't let it frustrate you. The more you work with these techniques and processes, the more you will figure out the little tricks that make them work for you. The only way to learn them is to do them repeatedly. We wish we could lean over your shoulder and encourage you, but we know you are up to the challenge.

Once all the rows are joined, it is time to set in the side triangle wedges. This will seem so easy after getting all the points of the stars set into all those diamonds! Mark the dot at the tip of the triangle for easy placement on the quilt top. These wedges are a little larger than needed to allow for trimming before adding borders. Position the dot at the intersecting seams; then pin and stitch toward the outside edge. Turn the triangle around to the other side and repeat, making a clean point at the intersection. Press toward the large triangle. Repeat for the remaining three wedges.

Next, add the four corner triangles. They are also a little large, so center them so you can square the corner when you trim the edges of the quilt top.

Check the top for even sides and square corners (Volume 1, Class 180, page 93). Add borders of your choice (Volume 1, Class 180, page 95). The easiest way to do this is to use an 8½″ × 24½″ ruler. Place the ¼″ line along the edge of the ruler on the outside points of the side wedges and draw a line. Using a large square ruler, square the corners, aligning the sides of the ruler with the drawn lines. Before cutting, measure the width in several places and then the length to ensure that the quilt is square and even before cutting. Trim once you have everything squared.

Choose what size and color variation you want for borders and add, using the guidelines in Volume 1, Class 180 (page 95). You have come a long way from the Rail Fence quilts in Volume 1! We hope you loved making this quilt top.

PROJECT TWO: *DIAMOND STARBURST*

Diamond Starburst

There are many fabrics in this quilt—18 different prints for the stars and a background. Harriet chose a very scrappy palette for this pattern. She found the background fabric first, and then Carrie spent a lot of time choosing fabrics that looked good with the background. Her goal for a very old-looking quilt was achieved by using very subtle color combinations. This pattern could easily be made using brights, batiks, or reproduction fabrics. Take some time to play with many bolts of fabric to come up with colors that please you.

This is a star that ends at the center round; the points of this round are cut off, which makes the star a hexagon block.

Quilt size: 70″ × 75″ (without borders)

Yardages needed:

2½ yards background (*does not* include border)

½ yard each of 18 different prints

The points of each star are made up of four strip sets and one single strip. Each strip set combination will accommodate one star. The strips are cut on the lengthwise grain of the fabric to minimize stretching. Each ½-yard piece will yield strips 18″ long.

> *note* Harriet did not plan the color positions for the stars before cutting the fabric. She cut all the fabric into strips and put them in piles, and then Carrie helped plan the color combinations. The required number of strips were then taken from the piles and positioned in the order that the strips would be sewn. There were quite a few strips left over, so if you want to be frugal with your fabric, design your stars and cut just what you need to accommodate each combination. Don't forget that you can interview your color placement choices using mirrors, as we showed in Class 420, Lesson Two (page 27).

For each star, cut:

   Round 1: 1 – 2″ × 18″ strip

   Round 2: 2 – 2″ × 18″ strips

   Round 3: 3 – 2″ × 18″ strips

   Round 4: 4 – 2″ × 18″ strips

   Round 5: 5 – 2″ × 18″ strips

Lay out the strips in the following order:

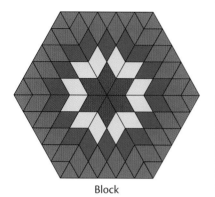

Block

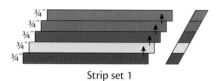

Strip set 1

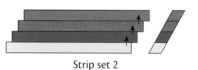

Strip set 2

Strip set 3

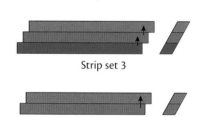

Strip set 4

Strip set 5

Once the strips are arranged in order, sew them together. Be sure to stagger the strips at the left end by ¾″. Remember to sew two strips together, press carefully, and starch lightly. Press all seams toward the outside (Round 5). Trim each strip on either side of the seam to exactly 1¾″ before adding the next strip. Be as careful and accurate as possible to ensure easy seam alignment when the segments are joined—it all starts here.

Once the pressing is completed, measure each strip set width. This step is critical to make sure that the strips are accurate so that the segments will fit together easily. If each of the strip sets doesn't measure 1½″ wide the entire length, the diamonds will not be accurate when cut, and the seams will not match easily. The finished widths of the strip sets are as follows:

Set 4: 3½″ wide

Set 3: 5″ wide

Set 2: 6½″ wide

Set 1: 8″ wide

> *tip* If it has been a while since you made the sample star from Lesson Three (page 36), we suggest that you make one star to start with to review the process of pressing, cutting, and so on, before starting on the quilt and then finding there is an accuracy problem.

Once all of the strip sets are sewn, pressed, trimmed, and measured, and everything is the correct size, it is time to cut them into 60° segments. You will need a large 60° triangle (we used the 8″ Creative Grids 60° Triangle Ruler) and a 2½″ × 12½″ ruler. Lay the strip set on your cutting mat with the outside round strip (Round 1) at the bottom. Trim the uneven ends on the left end of the strip set to a perfect 60° angle with the triangle ruler. Align the long bottom edge of the triangle ruler with the raw edge of the bottom strip. Cut along the left side of the angle, cutting off the offset ends of the strip set. Using the 2½″ ruler, measure 2″ from this new edge. Now position the triangle ruler so that the lines on the triangle are exactly aligned with the seamlines and the bottom edge of the strip set, and up against the right side

of the long ruler. Once everything is exactly measured and positioned, move the triangle ruler and cut the strip set. Move the ruler down 2″, check the angle again with the triangle ruler, move to the side, and cut. Cut each strip set into 6 units, constantly checking for the 60° alignment of the cut edge.

Close-up of ruler measuring 2″ at 60° (both rulers)

> *tip* Stack the strip sets from small (Round 5 on bottom) to large (Round 1 on top) in a pile. Cut the segments from the widest strip set first, then the next widest, and so on, until you get to the single strip. Stack the segments as you cut so they will be in the correct order for layout once all the cutting is done.

Once the units are cut, lay out one star beside the machine to form the piles of segments. The stack will have six segments in each, ready to chain-stitch together.

Stacks of segments for star points

To start, place the single diamond on top of the two-diamond unit, right sides together. The cut edge of the single diamond's corner is placed right at the seam of the bottom unit. Once this is in position, you will see the V at the end of the units where the needle exits.

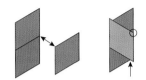

Alignment of first two segments

When you have all of the first two segments sewn together, align and sew the third and fourth segments together. Carefully press these seams open. Sew these two units together and press the seams open. Add the last segment—the longest—and press the seam open. Once all five segments are joined and pressed, place a 60° triangle ruler on top of each section to be sure each is still 60°. Correct by re-pressing or resewing if necessary. Are you amazed at how easily and perfectly these seams intersected?

Checking finished point with 60° ruler

These six sections will now be joined to make one star. Lay out the six points and construct three pairs, closely following the instructions given for the sample blocks made

earlier (page 38). Press the seams open as you go. Once you have three pairs of points, join them together into the star. If everything stayed accurate, the star will be flat and all seams will match exactly. Construct 18 star blocks total.

Six points coming together for each star

To trim the stars to get straight sides, use an 8″-wide ruler or large square. Position the ruler on the star, placing the 7¾″ ruler line on the seamline that runs through the star's center. Be sure that the points on the outside where you will be cutting are ¼″ from the edge of the ruler for the seam allowance. Continue around the block to trim all six sides of each star, keeping the 60° line of the ruler against each cut edge.

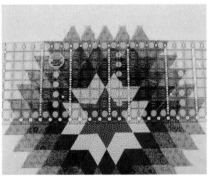

Ruler placement to trim points

From the background fabric, cut five 8¼″ × 45″ strips. You might need one more strip if your fabric is

a bit narrow and you can get only seven triangles per strip. Using your 60° triangle, cut 38 setting triangles. You will get seven or eight triangles per strip.

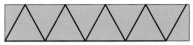

Cutting setting triangles from strips

Cut a length of fabric 32″ long and four equal widths (about 11″ wide) after removing the selvages. You will be cutting the 60° side wedges needed to fill in the sides of the quilt top. Fold each of the lengths in half lengthwise and make sure the edges are perfectly even and straight, or cut a clean edge ¼″ in from the raw edge.

Position the point of the 60° triangle at the fold (make sure to adjust if your ruler has a blunt point) and the center ruler line on the cut edge. Extend the angle created by the ruler with a long straightedge to the corner of the strip.

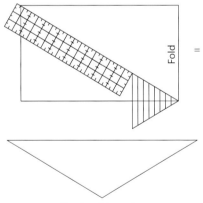

Cutting side wedge

Cut along the side of the rulers or draw a line and cut carefully on the line. When you open the fold after cutting, you will have a 60° side wedge. You need four of these. These wedges are a bit too long and wide, which will allow you to set them into place and trim them to a straight edge on the completed quilt top when it is finished. The triangles on the corners are also too large so that the corners can be squared before adding borders.

You are now ready to go to the design wall or a large floor and lay out the quilt top. There are two different ways to construct this top—in straight horizontal rows or in diagonal rows. You can choose which you want to do. Using the diagram, lay out all the stars and setting triangles. You will no doubt want to play around with the placement of the stars to get a good balance of the color combinations.

Layout in horizontal rows

Layout in diagonal rows

note Harriet chose to use the diagonal layout to piece her top together. Working down the rows, she added a triangle to two opposite sides of the stars in the center three rows. Once the seams were pressed, it was easy to match the intersecting points, pin in position, and sew the blocks together into a row.

Constructing rows

The top right and lower left corners are the same, with three triangles added to the stars, and the top star of Row 2 and the bottom star of Row 5 have the triangles located in different positions. Work carefully and pin the pieces into place at the design wall to avoid confusion and ripping.

Once the top is constructed, trim the sides and corners as you learned in Volume 1 (page 102). Add borders of your choice.

This is quite a stunning quilt, and we think once you have it done, you will be very impressed with yourself. You're now ready to venture into eight-pointed stars. The skills you learned here will be a huge asset as you get involved with designs that are more difficult.

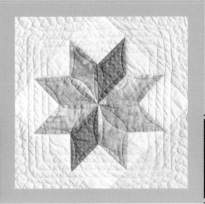

Class 440

We hope you had a good time working with the 60° diamonds in the first three classes. You are now venturing into the more difficult 45° diamonds and all the wonderful stars that are made from them. The most basic of the stars is the simple eight-pointed star, commonly known as the LeMoyne Star, which we will walk you through in this class. The basis of this star is the Y-seam, which strikes fear in many quilters. Many quilters never venture into this arena, thinking these stars are overly difficult to pull off. We think you will find that they are not that difficult once you learn the basics, just as you have found in every class throughout this series. We will start with the most basic stars and build on them until multipiece star points are taken in stride. Just remember that this type of piecing requires time and patience, so don't hurry or think these are "quilt in a day"–type designs. The time you put into them will reward you with breathtaking quilts!

LESSON ONE:
Basic drafting of the eight-pointed star

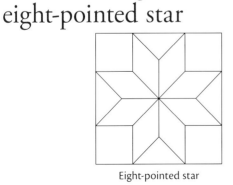

Eight-pointed star

The LeMoyne Star and other similar eight-pointed stars are not based on a grid. They are derived from eight identical diamonds spinning around a center point. If you imagine a circle divided into eight wedges, each wedge would be 45°. If the wedges are made of diamonds, you have an eight-pointed star. The diamonds have four equal sides and two pairs of parallel sides—known as true diamonds. There are different methods for drafting these stars, as explained in the upcoming sections. You will find that each method may result in a very small difference in the size of the units. The best way to determine which method is the most accurate is to make a block using each method and see which finished block is the closest to what you actually need. Method 1 will result in a block a bit smaller than 10″, and Methods 2 and 3 will be slightly larger than 10″.

METHOD 1

One of the easiest ways to draft the pattern units for simple eight-pointed stars is to draft one diamond based on the size of the block you want. We are using a 10″ block for our example.

Begin by dividing the block size (10″) by 2, and then divide that number by 2.414.

$$10 \div 2 = 5; 5 \div 2.414 = 2.07$$

Round that number to the nearest 1/8″, which is 2″ in this case. On a sheet of four-to-the-inch graph paper, draw two parallel lines that distance (2″) apart.

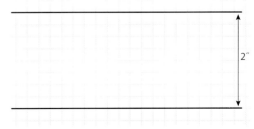

Draw two parallel lines on graph paper.

Establish a 45° angle, using a protractor or 45° triangle ruler, from the left end of the lower line.

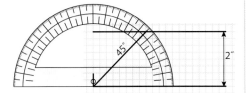

Use protractor to locate 45°angle.

With a straightedge ruler, draw a line to connect the end of the baseline to the marked 45° point on the upper line. Draw a second line 2″ away from that angled line. This completes the diamond.

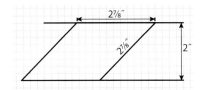

Measure down 2″ and draw another 45° line.

This diamond is your pattern for drafting eight identical star points. Add ¼″ seam allowances around the outside edges to make a template or a rotary cutting guide.

To complete the LeMoyne Star, you need four corner squares and four side triangles.

For the corner squares, multiply the width of the diamond by 1.414 and then add ½″ for seam allowances. For our 10″ square, it would be:

2″ × 1.414 = 2.83″ (round up to 2⅞″); 2⅞″ + ½″ = 3⅜″

This is the size to cut the corner squares.

For the side triangles, multiply the finished width of the star point by 2 and add 1¼″ for seam allowances:

2″ × 2 = 4″; 4″ + 1¼″ = 5¼″

Cut one square 5¼″ and then cut it in half diagonally in both directions.

This will ensure that the straight grain of each triangle is on the outside edge of the block.

We have included this method because it is really basic and easy to follow. The following methods require more math, but we believe they are more accurate.

METHOD 2

Method 1 is simple, but it does not provide a line drawing of the basic octagonal shape to use if you want to divide any sections of the block into smaller or different shapes. Let's learn to draft a simple octagonal pattern and a basic eight-pointed star.

You would normally start by drawing a square on graph paper the size you want your block to be. But for demonstration purposes to learn the basics, we will start with a 4″ square. Make a mark in the center of the square 2″ from each side. Visualize a line from this center mark to one corner; label this line "r."

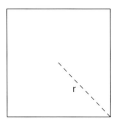

Finding first measurement

Using a compass set at the length of "r," make a mark on each side from all four corners. There will be eight marks. Connect these divisions by horizontal and vertical lines. Label each line, going around the square clockwise, with A through H. Starting with A, draw a line to the D mark. Continue by drawing lines between E and H, C and F, and B and G.

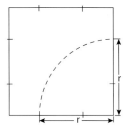

Use compass to find distances.

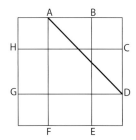

Basic eight-pointed star grid

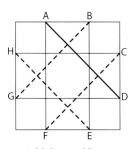

Add diagonal lines.

You will see two squares in the center overlapping one another. Draw diagonal lines corner to corner in both of these squares.

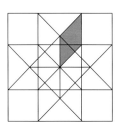

Intersecting center squares

Erase all lines except the sides of the star points and the diagonal lines inside the center squares. Now you have a basic drafting of an eight-pointed star. From this basic pattern, you can start to divide the points into different patterns. Here are a few that we will be discussing and making in Class 450. Do you see where the patterns/templates come from?

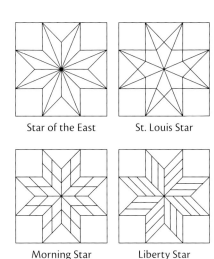

Star of the East   St. Louis Star

Morning Star   Liberty Star

METHOD 3

Math basics for drafting eight-pointed stars

The next two methods are more mathematically based. These methods give you the sizes of each pattern unit without drafting them on paper—instead using a calculator. Harriet learned these methods of drafting eight-pointed stars from Sharyn Craig, who knows drafting backward and forward. Sharyn coined the term *magic numbers* (we call them *basic measurements*); when you combine them with a calculator and an easy formula, you can make blocks in any size you choose.

If you study the dimensions of the LeMoyne Star, you will find that the side of a diamond is equal to the side of the square in the block. It is also equal to the side of the triangle. Once you find the actual measurement of any one of these units, you will know the measurements of the other two units.

If you remember the basic drafting concepts of triangles you learned in Volume 2 (page 24), you will recall that the diagonal of a square equals 1.414 times its side measurement.

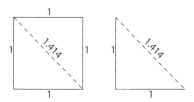

Finding diagonal measurement

Looking at one side of the block, you find two squares and a triangle. The triangle measurement is the diagonal of the corner square, which is 1.414 times its side measurement. Using the theorem, assign a value of 1 to the squares; "1" always represents the side of the square, the side of the diamond, and the side of the triangle. Assign a value of 1.414 to the triangle; "1.414" always represents the base of the triangle and the distance between the points of the stars. Notice that the distance between the points of the diamonds is the same as the base of the triangle.

When you total the units that are positioned along one outer edge side of the block, they add up to 3.414. This number can be used with a calculator to determine the sizes of the pattern pieces for any size LeMoyne Star block you need. If you divide the size of the block you want (12″) by the sum of the parts (12″ ÷ 3.414 = 3.515″ = 3½″), the resulting number—the basic measurement—is the finished size of the corner square, which is also the size of all four sides of the diamond and the two short sides of the triangle.

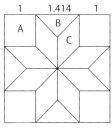

LeMoyne Star formula

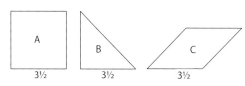

Template pieces and measurements

Begin by choosing the size of finished block you want. Divide the block size by the "basic measurement" (3.414) to get the side measurement of the square, diamond, and triangle. Round that number up to the nearest ⅛″. Add ¼″ seam allowances to all sides to determine what size to cut the pieces.

Let's work through the formula using a 12″ block:

12″ (block size) ÷ 3.414 = 3.51″ (3½″) = finished corner size

Add ¼″ seam allowances to all sides. This relates to each piece as follows:

Corner squares = 3½″ + ½″ for seam allowances = 4″ cut squares

Diamonds = 2½″ + ½″ seam allowance = 3″-wide and -long diamonds

Side triangles = 5″ + 1¼″ seam allowance = 6.25″ = template with the two straight sides measuring 4⅜″, or a 6¼″ square cut in half diagonally both directions

METHOD 4

The process of Method 3 can be reversed by choosing the finished size of the pattern pieces and then determining the size of the block. Choose a finished size for the pattern pieces that is easy to cut. Multiply that number by the "magic number" (3.414) to determine the finished block size. Round that number up to the nearest ⅛".

As an example, let's use 3":

3" (finished size of pieces) × 3.414 = 10.24" or 10¼" block

A 10¼" block may seem like an odd size, but if all the blocks in the quilt are the same size, it doesn't matter what size they are. If you are designing a quilt from scratch and there are different blocks in the design, you may have to resign yourself to working with more difficult numbers when cutting to get all the blocks into workable measurements.

We suggest that you take the time to work through these different methods so that you understand the diamond and how it is cut, as well as the options you have for making blocks of different sizes. We will return to these processes in Class 450, where the 45° diamonds are used in more complex blocks. Knowing how to draft them is key, as there are very few patterns on the market for these wonderful blocks. If you do find a pattern, it is seldom the size you want.

Before we leave these ideas, let's look at Feathered Stars. Several stars are drafted around an eight-pointed star in the center. If you enjoyed learning to make Feathered Stars in Volume 3 (pages 90–108), this is a good way to expand your repertoire of these elegant blocks. Here is an example of a few of them.

Feathered Stars with LeMoyne Star in centers

If you start to get more interested in the concept of drafting complex blocks and want a deeper understanding of the underlying structure of the blocks, we highly recommend Sally Collins's book *Drafting for the Creative Quilter,* published by C&T Publishing.

Basic Y–seam process for constructing eight-pointed stars

Before we begin, we want to give full credit to Sharyn Craig for the method of making LeMoyne Stars you are going to learn. In our opinion, it is the most straightforward process and has the highest potential for success. We think you will fall in love with these stars once you see how easy they are to make. The success, however, is due to accuracy in cutting, sewing, and pressing, so don't let your guard down here. Work carefully and you will be amazed!

We suggest that you cut out one star, using the measurements given, from scrap fabric and work through the process before you begin making stars from project fabric. We also suggest that you try rotary cutting a first star, and then making another using templates for the cutting. We tend to prefer templates for these stars, as the pieces seem to be more accurate. This will be your choice once you see the results from both.

We will start by making a 12" LeMoyne Star. This size is large enough to handle easily while you are learning the process of Y-seams. Once you have the system down, we will move on to 6" stars, which is a size for which you will find many uses.

For the 12" star, we like to use Perfect Patchwork Templates, Set E, pieces #30, #31, and #32. If you do not have these templates, you can draft your own 12" LeMoyne Star using any of the methods given earlier (page 51). Make your own templates or rotary cut the following sizes. *We want to stress the importance of cutting accurately when working with these angles.*

Cut:

    4 – 4" squares of background fabric

    1 – 6¼" square of background fabric, cut in half diagonally in both directions for the side triangles

    8 – 3" diamonds (strip is cut 3" wide; cut a 45° angle, move ruler down 3" and cut another 45° angle)

You do not have to mark the corner dots with the system we are using. Other construction methods might require you to sew dot to dot, but this method does not.

Start by laying all the pieces into the star block on the right side of your machine before beginning to sew. This will keep a visual image of the star in front of you and help keep confusion to a minimum.

Units positioned at side of machine

Next, divide the star into sub-units. Stack the matching pieces of all four sub-units. You will construct all four at the same time.

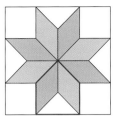

Sub-unit position within block

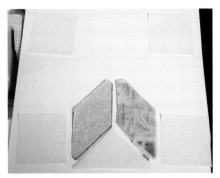

Sub-units stacked

Pick up the triangle on the top of the stack and place it on top of the left-hand diamond, with right sides together and the two edges exactly aligned. If you cut with the Perfect Patchwork Templates, make sure the corner cuts are aligned exactly.

Stitch triangle to left diamond.

Keeping the triangle on top, sew from edge to edge toward the point of the triangle. The first seam of a Y-seam unit will always be sewn edge to edge. Do not clip the threads or remove the unit from the machine. Continue to chainstitch the remaining three triangle and diamond pieces.

Clip the units apart and press each seam allowance toward the diamond. Return the units to the same position they were in before sewing, where the remaining diamond is.

Pick up one of the units you just completed and place the remaining diamond right sides together with the triangle, again aligning the points of both exactly and making sure the edges are perfectly even.

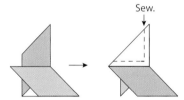

Place second diamond on top of triangle.

Turn the unit over so that the triangle is on top and you can see the previously sewn seam. Sew from the edge of the triangle to the stitching and stop. Be careful not to go one stitch beyond the stitching. This line of stitching should end exactly at the end of the previously sewn seam. If the seams do not come to the same point, check your cutting and/or the alignment of the edges and try again. Repeat with the remaining three units. Press seam allowances toward the diamond.

Next, fold one unit in half, right sides together, and align the edges of the diamonds. The triangle will be folded in half. Be sure that the points of the diamonds and the triangles, as well as all the outside edges, are even. Pin in place if you feel the need to hold the layers together tightly.

Fold unit in half, and pull seam allowance toward triangle.

Pull the triangle seam allowance down and out of the way before sewing. Sew this seam from the outer edge of the diamond point down to the previous stitching. Repeat with the remaining three units. Clip apart and open. Press seam allowances toward the right diamond, working from the right side of the unit.

Back and front of pressed unit

On the front side of each sub-unit, the point should be flat and square. If it has a little tuck, the stitching did not stop soon enough or the edges were not aligned exactly. Pick out the stitches and try again. These units are the basis for the rest of the block, and if they are not accurate, the rest of the block will not be accurate.

Stack the sub-units with the triangle at the bottom to the side of the machine. To the right of this stack, make a stack of the corner squares. Pick up one square and place it right sides together with the first diamond unit of the stack. Match the edge of the square exactly with the edge of the triangle. If these edges are not

exact, there will not be a ¼″ seam allowance beyond the point of the star along the edge of the block. Sew edge to edge with the square on top. Repeat with the remaining three units in each stack. Press seams toward the square.

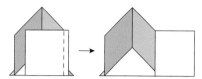

Place square on top of sub-unit.

These units will be stacked again, but only two per stack, positioned as shown.

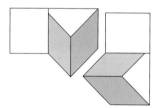

Position units.

Place the unit on the right on top of the left unit, right sides together. Match the edges of the top square to the edge of the triangle and the diamond. Stitch from the outer edge toward the previous stitching. Stop exactly at the previous stitching. Repeat with the second pair of units. Press these seams toward the diamond. When you turn the block over to the back, all the seams should be spinning clockwise. If they are not, go back and re-press. This will be the last time you can make any changes.

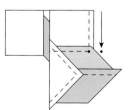

Stitch from outer edge.

With right sides together, butt the diamond seams of the sub-units

together and align the outside edges of the triangles and the diamonds on both sides, making sure the square is folded in half exactly. The diamond points need to be the same length and butted right up to the end. Pin these strategic places to help hold them in alignment.

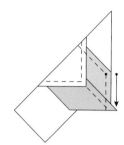

Sew two diamonds together.

Stitch from the outside edge of the point to the seamline at the square. Open the unit and check that the square corner is flat and square, and the diamond points are intersecting correctly. This is very much like making pinwheels with half-square triangles, as we did in Volume 3, Class 320 (page 29). If these seams are not making perfect points, take the seam out and try again. If these points aren't aligned properly, you won't be able to have an accurate center to the star.

Point alignment on right side of unit

You are almost there! Three more seams to go. Lay these units on the table in position to make the star block. You can see the seams that need to be joined. Take your time to position these correctly before sewing. It is easy to get the wrong edges sewn together. You are going to sew the remaining edge of the square to the diamond of the opposite unit.

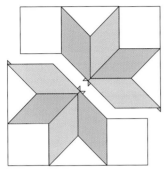

Last seam of corners

Flip the upper unit over the lower unit and pin this seam in place. Again, make sure all the outside edges are exactly aligned so that you have the needed ¼″ seam allowance beyond the star points on the outside edges of the block.

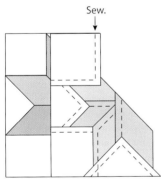

Sew last seam of square, and pull seam allowance toward diamond.

Start at the outside edge and stitch just to the seamline, pulling the seam allowance back out of the way. Repeat for the opposite corner—but before sewing, lay out the block flat again to be sure you have the correct edges going together. Press these seam allowances toward the diamonds.

If everything has been aligning properly so far, this last seam should be a cinch. The last seam is the center of

the block. Fold the block in half and align the raw edges.

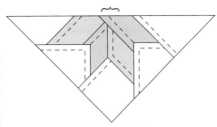

Fold block in half.

Begin by matching all the points at the center. Make sure all the diamond tips finish at the same point. All seam allowances should be alternating at the center, allowing you to butt corresponding seams around the star. Pin these in place to hold the block square.

Your checkpoints are as follows:

❋ The internal diamond seams are butting together.

❋ The outside edges are straight and aligned with each other.

❋ The center seam is straight.

❋ The point intersections are all the same distance from the center raw edge and align on top of one another accurately.

We suggest you baste the seam for about 2″ through the center to check your point alignment. Basting is much easier to take out if the points are not in the proper position. If they are correct, you can simply stitch over the basting.

To baste, set your stitch length at 4 or 5 and stitch about 1″ on either side of the center. Take the piece off the machine and open to the front side. Check that all eight points are coming together exactly. If they aren't, take out the basting, realign the points, and try again. It may take a couple

of tries to get this right. Once you are satisfied, shorten your stitch length and stitch from the seamline at the corner through the center to the seamline of the opposite corner.

Fan the seam allowances at the center by working them with your fingers so that all the seam allowances lie in the same clockwise motion as the rest of the seams. This will help the block to lie flat. You can press this last seam open if it helps the center to flatten. Press from the front. If the block is a bit out of square, spray with starch and iron into shape.

Back of completed block

Front of completed block

Closely examine your first LeMoyne Star block. If you had trouble and are not happy with it, learn from your mistakes and make another one. We are moving on to 6″ blocks, so if you are having trouble with the 12″ block, you might get really frustrated with the little ones. If your 12″ block turned out really well, you are apt to find the 6″ blocks fun and fairly quick as you make more and more of them.

6" LeMoyne Stars

This lesson is short on space but long on time to sew. We give you the cutting requirements for 6" stars, but we prefer that you draft your own using the instructions for the three different methods in Lesson One (page 49). Once you have your pieces cut, construct the small stars in the same manner as the 12" block in Lesson Two (page 52). These pieces are much smaller, making the work a bit fussy, but the stars are so adaptable when done. You might want to spend some time to make enough for the quilt in this class.

For 6" LeMoyne Stars, you can use Set E of the Perfect Patchwork Templates again, this time using templates #33, #34, and #35, or you can rotary cut all the pieces.

If rotary cutting, you will need:

2¼"-wide strip of background, cut into 2¼" squares (4 per block)

3¾"-wide strip of background, cut into squares and cut in half diagonally in both directions

1¾" strip of each diamond color

> *tip* To cut the diamonds as accurately as possible with rotary cutting methods, use the same process we used for 60° diamonds in Class 420 (page 21). Once the strip is cut, establish the 45° angle on the left end of the strip using a half-square triangle ruler or the Precision Trimmer 6 used throughout Volume 3. Align the ruler along the side of the strip and cut the 45° angle. Place your 2½" rotary ruler at the 1¾" line on this cut end and check the angle with the triangle ruler. Once everything is exact, move the triangle ruler and cut the strip. If the angle of the diamond is off in the least, the star will not finish flat and square. Double-check with each cut.

If you really want to have fun with these blocks, try working with a narrow-striped fabric. The smaller the stripe, the more variations you will be able to get.

If you look at quilt photos, especially photos of antique quilts, you will start to see these stars show up in many applications. Once you learn that they are not hard to make, you might want to add them to your quilt designs in different ways. Below is a list of ideas of how to use these blocks.

 ❋ Set the blocks in a straight set, side by side.

 ❋ Set the blocks on point, side by side.

 ❋ Use them in a straight set with sashing.

 ❋ Use them in a diagonal set with sashing.

 ❋ Alternate your star blocks with solid squares, either straight set or diagonal, with or without sashing. This is a quick way to make your quilt larger without having to piece many more star blocks.

 ❋ Use the 6" stars as cornerstones for different quilt designs.

 ❋ Use the 6" stars as the centers of larger blocks, even Log Cabins.

Go back to Volume 2 and play with the setting worksheets to help you generate ideas.

LESSON FOUR:

Working with and/or building your stash

This is a perfect time to talk about building a stash, as 6" LeMoyne Stars are perfect candidates for scrappy quilts. The points can be all one fabric, two alternating fabrics, or a different fabric for each point. When working with these types of blocks, drawing on a collection of fabric is much easier that going out and trying to purchase many small yardages that work together.

By this volume, we assume that you have been bitten by the fabric bug and have a hard time resisting those fabrics that you run across that you just *have* to have, even though you have no idea what you are going to do with them. A few shopping trips like this and you are well on your way to building a stash. Harriet actually refers to hers as her fabric collection, which at this point (35 years of quilting) is truly an amazing collection of reproduction fabrics. Carrie, though quilting for just a few years, has a considerable stash also. She grew up in a quilt shop from age 4 and often worked for fabric.

So, once you have the fabric, what do you do with it? You will find that eventually you will feel that you need to use some of it to justify having so much. The problem is how you have stored it and how easy it is to work with. We are going to give you some ideas on how to sort things out, organize, and get ready to use your treasure.

Sorting and organizing is the starting point. Sort your fabric by color so you know what you have and what colors are missing. You might want to sub-sort into themes, eras, and types of fabrics. Examples would be children's prints, Christmas prints, florals, batiks, 1840 reproductions, Civil War–era fabrics, and so on. If you don't have shelves that can hold all the fabric you have, you might want to invest in file drawers or plastic storage bins for storing your fabric.

We find the most fun in sorting fabric is that our imaginations run away with us. We start to combine colors and textures, wondering what kind of pattern would make these fabrics look their best. If you really like the combination, keep them together and keep an eye out for a pattern that you think would work, or start to design your own ideas into reality.

If you have a collection of patterns that you have wanted to make, now is a good time to pull the fabrics that you would like for a pattern and set them aside with the pattern. How often do you have a great idea, but when you go to put it together, you can't find that one fabric on the shelves that you know is there—and the idea won't work without it? Just think of the sewing time wasted during the hunt. Make up your own "kits" as you are organizing and you will have enough projects to keep you busy for a while.

We also find quite a few fabrics that we no longer care for. These are put aside to reconsider later or to donate to the local quilt guild. There is no reason to keep fabrics that we bought years ago but no longer like. Our tastes do change, and we move on. Years ago, when Harriet became obsessed by early-nineteenth-century quilts, she started collecting reproduction fabrics and steadily got rid of the more contemporary fabrics in her studio. She has never regretted it, as it takes every inch she can come up with to store her ever-growing collection of nineteenth-century reproduction fabrics. This collection of reproduction fabrics spans 25 years and is a constant source of inspiration for making the quilts of that era.

Harriet's fabric wall

Reproduction fabrics are a one-shot deal. Unlike fabrics like marbles and polka dots, each reproduction print and colorway is offered once and for a limited amount of time. Fabric companies have lines that span 20–40 years within a line. To stay true to the replication of an antique, it takes many fabrics of an era. It would be impossible to go to a store and find enough variety at one time, in the same era, to pull off a true reproduction quilt. Without a stash, you would be limited to the possibilities available. What better reason to buy and store fabric!

You might also want to separate out fabrics that are large prints and border stripes. Large prints are a true inspiration as jumping-off points for color combination ideas or great borders.

You can see that working with your stash and building a working stash is like money in the bank. If you start to use these fabrics, you won't feel quite so guilty when you just can't resist that new piece in the store. You are just replenishing!

We can't leave this subject without addressing those pesky scraps that mound up. We feel guilty throwing them away if they are of any size, but how do we control them?

The quilts we are getting into as we progress through this series of books lend themselves more and more to the use of scraps. Star blocks especially look much more interesting with a variety of fabrics used throughout the project. So how do we manage scraps?

The best time to set up a system for managing scraps is when you start quilting. Once you have quilted for years, the scraps can present a daunting task of sorting. We suggest that you sort your scraps into three different piles. The first pile is the large pieces, the leftover quarter yards, partial pieces of fat quarters, and so on. Clean up the edges, press, and fold neatly.

The second pile is made up of the leftover strips from all the projects you've made. There are always leftover strips from 2″ to 4″ wide or often the full width of the fabric. These are very usable scraps.

Pile three is all the smaller pieces— leftover half-square triangles, flying geese units, odd-shaped cuttings, and so on. These pieces are small enough that they need to be cut one by one into a shape to use in a quilt. Press them and, if you are ambitious, precut them into the largest size square or triangle you can make them into. If this seems overwhelming, sort them by size, and then go even further and sort by color.

As you get more and more scraps, keep them organized as you go. You are apt to find just what you need for that one block in your current project—especially if it is a scrap quilt.

Happy collecting and sorting!

LESSON FIVE:

The quilt

PROJECT ONE: *SPRING GARDEN*

Spring Garden

This quilt was inspired by a line of fabrics that came into our store. The multicolored print inspired the color choices and became four of the eight points in each star. Five colors were taken from this print for the other points. A medium and light of each color were used for fun. A common diagonal set allowed us

to use two colors in the side-setting triangles, which appear as an inside border of sorts. The border print brings it all together. The small brown border on both sides of the print is part of the border print.

The instructions are light for this quilt, as we expect you to know the basics of this set and how to piece the side-setting triangles from working through *Quilter's Academy Volume 2*, or at least be able to refer back to previous lessons for a refresher.

Quilt top size: 51″ × 62½″ (without borders); 67″ × 78½″ (with borders)

Block size: 9″

Blocks: 20

Yardages needed:

⅛ yard each of light purple, yellow, green, peach, and blue

⅛ yard each of medium purple, yellow, green, peach, and blue

⅔ yard multicolor print for stars

1 yard background for stars

1 yard background for alternate blocks

⅞ yard green for side-setting triangles

¼ yard brown for side-setting triangles

2¼ yards border print (if there are four repeats across width of fabric)

Using the instructions in Lesson One (page 49), draft a basic 9″ LeMoyne Star. Once the star is drafted, measure the pieces and add seam allowances to obtain your cutting measurements. You will be working with a couple of ⅛″ measurements when you cut, so watch your ruler carefully when cutting the pieces. We found it helpful to make a template for the side triangles, as it was difficult to stay accurate with a rotary ruler.

Cut:

  80 background squares

  80 background triangles

  80 multicolored diamonds

  8 each of all the medium and light colors for the star points

Following the instructions in Lesson Two (page 52), construct twenty LeMoyne Star blocks, making four each of the five color combinations. Once each block is finished, check that it is 9½″ square.

Cut twelve 9½″ squares from the second background for the alternate blocks. Now it is time to go to the design wall. Position the blocks on point and play with the color placement until you like the way the colors are scattered throughout the quilt top. Lay in the alternate blocks between the stars. Refer back to Volume 2, Class 230 (page 22), if you need assistance in the diagonal set layout process.

The side-setting triangles can be pieced, as we made them, or just plain triangles. If you choose to have plain triangles, refer to the formula for sizing and cutting, again in Volume 2, Class 230, Lesson Two (page 23). We gave instructions for adding strips to side-setting triangles in Volume 2 (page 98) but have found that the method uses a lot of fabric for the size of the point added to this quilt. Instead, we have found it is better to work with squares and add the brown triangles onto the larger triangles after they are cut.

You will need to cut four 14″ squares of the green triangle fabric. Cut these squares into quarters diagonally. You need fourteen side-setting triangles. Cut four 7″ squares of the brown fabric for the small triangles. Cut these squares into quarters diagonally. Draw a line on the right side of the fabric, 3¾″ from the long edge of the green triangle. Use a water-soluble marking tool for this line, as you don't want it to show if you miss it a bit. This is the sewing line for the brown triangle. Position the brown triangle on top of the green triangle, right sides together and seamlines matching.

Position of small triangle

Stitch ¼″ from the raw edge of the brown triangle. Press and then trim away the point of the green triangle that is underneath the brown triangle. Once this is done, you might want to use the corner of a large square ruler to check that the point is still a true 90° angle. If it isn't, trim to make a perfectly square corner.

Once the side-setting triangles are made, add them to your design wall. Now you are ready to assemble the blocks into rows and then the rows into your top.

Layout of quilt top

Once the top is assembled and pressed well, it is time to square it to make ready for the borders. Again, we are going to send you back to Volume 2, Class 280, Lesson One (page 96), where this process was taught. We mitered the corners so that the brown stripe would continue around the quilt. If you need instructions, refer to Volume 1, Class 180, Lesson Four (page 98).

We hope that you are starting to enjoy the amount of knowledge and skill you have gained as you have worked through each of the *Quilter's Academy* volumes. Use these books as reference books and you can create anything!

As you continue to Class 450, you will be learning many variations of the eight-pointed stars. These stars are addictive and actually easy to construct once you get the system down.

Class 450

Designing with eight-pointed stars

Now that you have mastered making LeMoyne Stars, we are going to mix it up and add pieces within and around each point to create more dynamic designs. Many of these patterns go by different names, so we provide a gallery of blocks for you to study to get familiar with the shapes and configurations of each. Granted, this is just a sampling of all the eight-pointed star variations out there, but we have chosen the most common or the ones we think are appropriate to your skill level and fun to make. It was hard to know where to stop, as there are so many variations of these blocks. They can get very complex, and we hope that by working through some or all of these, you will be up to the challenge of pushing yourself to try increasingly complicated blocks. The quilts in Volume 6 will be using complicated blocks and settings, as that will be your PhD year. Be prepared to win ribbons from here on in with your quilts when you use these types of designs. They are becoming less frequently seen, as the skills taught to the majority of quilters are not up to this level.

GALLERY OF EIGHT-POINTED STAR BLOCKS

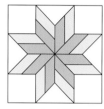

Striped Star

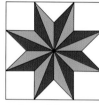
Star of the East (Divided Star)

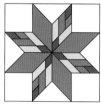
Formosa Tea Leaf (North Star)

Dove in the Window

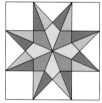

St. Louis Star

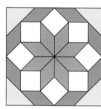
Rolling Star

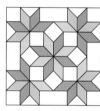
Snow Crystals (Yankee Pride)

Carpenter's Wheel (Double Star)

We have given you a line drawing of each of these patterns to play with colors and placement ideas. If you feel the urge to play with fabrics and colors as you look at these blocks, don't forget about using mirrors. Auditioning with mirrors can give you a good idea of color placement and choosing fabrics for the outside setting pieces. Place the mirrors at the narrow point of one mock-up block to see the multiplied image. Move the mirrors to the opposite wider point for a totally different perspective. Often stripes that are cut and mitered for the corner squares can give a really striking frame affect. Place the mirrors so that they intersect the corner squares diagonally on a square cut from a stripe. The use of darks and lights can really change a block depending on their position. You might want to take digital photos of each image and compare the possibilities. It is much easier to change a diagram than to rip out blocks and start over.

Once you have some ideas, go back to Volume 2, Class 250 (page 54) and start to play with the layout worksheets to see the setting potential of your block.

LESSON TWO:

Drafting more complex eight-pointed stars with graph paper

This lesson illustrates each of the blocks in Lesson One and works through the basic numbers and various sizes so you get a feel for how to determine the block size and/or the template size.

Striped Star, Star of the East, Formosa Tea Leaf, Dove in the Window, and St. Louis Star are all like LeMoyne Star, only they have points made from more than one piece sewn together to make the diamonds. These design elements do not affect the drafting, so we won't repeat the process here. This is fully covered in Class 440, Lesson One (page 49). Once you understand how to use the calculator to determine the sizes needed for the various templates for each block, the system becomes easier and easier. The use of the "1" and "1.414" values is the key. Just as you added those values together for the simpler eight-pointed stars and came up with 3.41, you will analyze the following blocks to see how to use those values to determine the sizes of templates needed for any size block.

Before we get into the calculator math of these blocks, we want to go through the breakout of the internal parts to make understanding the math easier. For many, drafting on graph paper makes more sense. Math is not visual in a calculator answer.

Continuing from Class 440, Lesson Two (page 52), we will now work with the same basic eight-pointed star, finding the divisions using a compass. Once the marks are made on your square, instead of drawing horizontal and vertical lines, connect adjacent octagonal lines.

Octagonal lines drawn in

Label the dividing points a to h clockwise around the block. Draw a horizontal and a vertical line through the center of the square and label these A to D clockwise around the square.

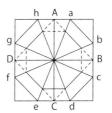

Labeling dividing points

Draw lines to connect ae, bf, cg, and dh. These lines join the diagonally opposing octagonal divisions through the center. Also connect the midpoint of the sides of the square—AB, BC, CD, and DA. The last lines connect ab, cd, ef, and gh. This block is known as Spiderweb and is an excellent starting point for diagonal divisions of an octagonal block.

Spiderweb

A different block appears when you change where the lines are drawn. Complete the first two steps for Spiderweb. To find the midpoints along the sides, you will use a compass. Lightly draw in one diagonal line of the square. Starting in a corner on the diagonal line, adjust your compass to the distance from the corner to the octagonal line (a). Mark this distance, using the compass, on the remaining seven sides of the octagon to find the midpoints (b). This same measurement equally bisects the line from the center (O) to the corner. OC is equal to the setting of the compass. Putting the point of your compass in the center (O), make a mark on the eight axis lines. Draw in the lines to develop the pattern.

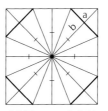

Establishing equal divisions

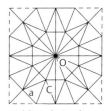

Adding design lines

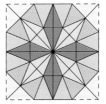

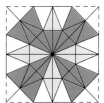

Evening Star color variations

Snow Crystals is the first block we will address with calculator math. But before we do, we want to explain the initial breakout of the block, as there is now a central square involved, and we want you to know how to draft the block on graph paper.

The next concept in star pattern drafting is making up a design from four identical quadrants. The easiest way to locate the central square is to draw the diagonals of a block and then draw lines connecting the midpoints of the sides. This works regardless of the size of the block or whether it has even- or odd-numbered measurements. To find the center square, connect the intersections of lines A, B, C, and D. Many times finding the center square will instantly indicate the easiest way to draft a pattern.

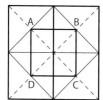
Finding center square

To draft Snow Crystals with this method, draw a square on graph paper and then locate and draw in the center square. Draft an eight-pointed star in the center square using the methods you learned in Class 440. Continue drafting portions of eight-pointed stars in the four corner quadrants.

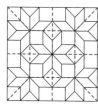
Snow Crystals

You could have technically located all the needed templates just from the star in the center square or in any one quadrant. We know that the central square is equal to one-fourth of the total block, so just drawing the center and one corner would be all you need.

We are going to do one more—the Carpenter's Wheel, also known as Dutch Rose, Double Star, Broken Star, or Star and Diamond. You will see that the templates are found in the same way as for Snow Crystals, and you really don't have to draft the entire block. However, we think it is a good idea to see how all these pieces come together on paper.

Start by finding the central square. Draft the eight-pointed star within it. Connect the midpoints on all four sides to establish the corner triangles.

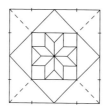
Drawing in star and corner triangles

Subdivide the corner triangles by connecting the octagonal division lines. Draw a second central square within the first one by connecting the octagonal divisions of the first square.

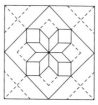
Further dividing block

Draw vertical and horizontal lines to develop the corners and side diamonds. Align the ruler with the midpoint of the subline in the corner triangles and the point of the square made from the inner central square.

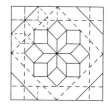
Adding vertical and horizontal lines

Add the remaining lines needed to complete the block. We have drawn in one corner with red so that you can see what the ruler lines up with to complete the small diamonds around the center.

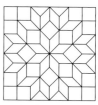
Finished block

Whew! Are you thinking you are back in a basic geometry class? If drawing and measuring are not your cup of tea, perhaps you will like the calculator math better. We find that we need to know both to have the freedom to draft and make any block we want. As you get further and further into designing your own quilts, you will find that these skills will come to your rescue many times.

LESSON THREE:
Calculator drafting

Let's start with Snow Crystals. Now that you have seen how it is broken apart on paper from the previous lesson, you will be able to see the units in the block more easily than before.

tip We have added a quick reference chart as a reminder of how much seam allowance to add when drafting and rotary cutting. You have learned all these measurements throughout Volumes 1–3, but you might find it handy to have them close by when calculating sizes and adapting your answers to rotary-cut sizes, as well as all the odd shapes you will encounter later on.

Add-on seam allowance chart

Square	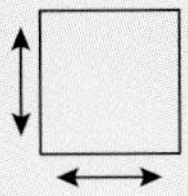	Add ½″ to the height and ½″ to the length of the desired finished size.
Half-square triangle	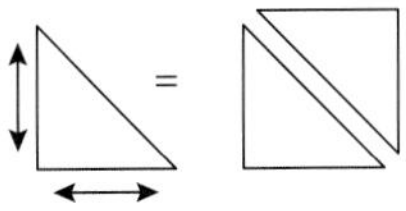	A half-square triangle is a square cut in half once diagonally. Add ⅞″ to the desired finished size of one short side of the triangle. Cut a square this size and cut it in half.
Quarter-square triangle	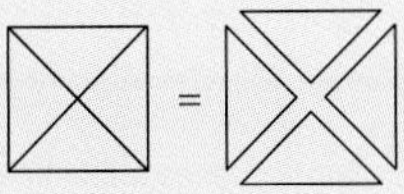	A quarter-square triangle is a square cut in half diagonally twice. Add 1¼″ to the desired finished size of the longest side of the quarter-square triangle.
True rectangle	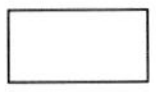	A true rectangle is twice as long as it is high. Add ½″ to the height and ½″ to the length of the desired finished size.
Half-rectangle from a true rectangle	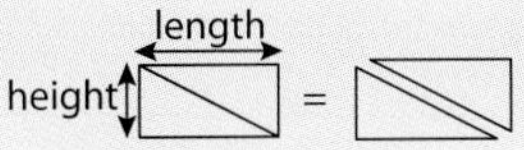	Half-rectangles are made by cutting a rectangle in half diagonally. For a true half-rectangle, add 1¹⁄₁₆″ to the height and 1⁵⁄₁₆″ to the length of the desired finished size.
60° equilateral triangle	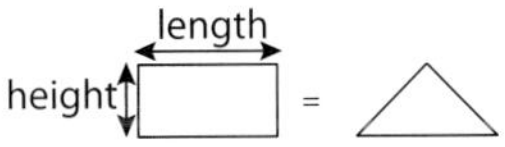	Equilateral triangles have three sides of equal length and are cut from a true rectangle. Add ¾″ to the height and ⅞″ to the length of the desired finished size.
45° diamond	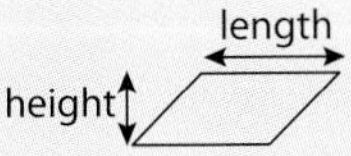	The height determines the cutting width. Add ½″ to the height and ½″ to the length.
60° diamond	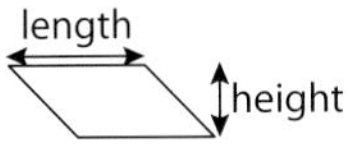	The height determines the cutting width. Add ½″ to the height and ½″ to the length.
Parallelogram	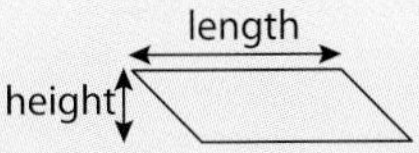	A parallelogram is a rectangle with both ends cut at the same angle so it looks like an elongated diamond. The width of the diagonal cut will never be the same as the height of the strip. Add ½″ to the height and ¾″ to the length of the desired finished size. Turn the ruler diagonally to find the width of the diagonal cuts.
Full trapezoid	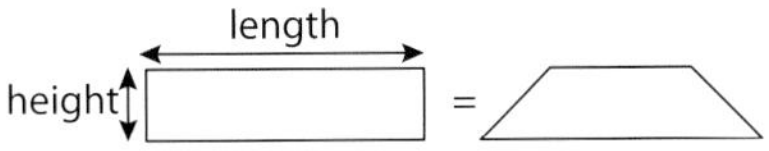	A full trapezoid is a rectangle with both ends cut off at opposite angles—usually 45°. Add 1½″ to the height and 1¼″ to the length of the desired finished size.
Left or right half-trapezoid	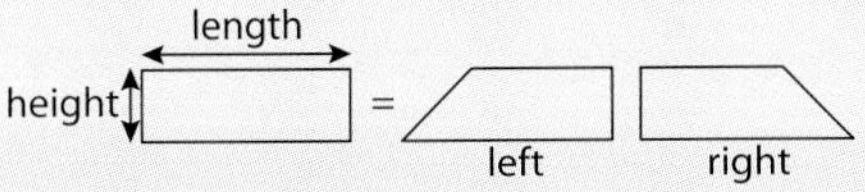	This is a rectangle with only one end cut at an angle. Add ½″ to the height and ⅞″ to the length of the desired finished size.
Double prism	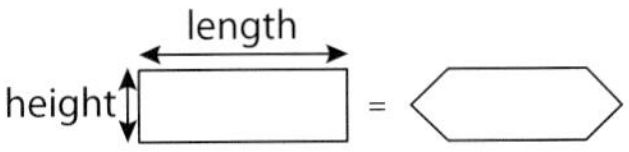	This is cut from a rectangle. Add ½″ to the height and ¾″ to the length of the desired finished size.
Prism	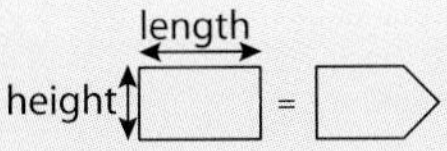	This is a rectangle with one end cut into a point made of 45° angles. Add ½″ to the height and ⅝″ to the length of the desired finished size.
Kite shape		The kite shape is a half-square triangle with one tip cut off so it is symmetrical. The two short sides are equal in length, and the two long sides are equal in length. Add ⅞″ to the desired finished length of the long side of the kite shape. Cut a square this size. Cut the square in half diagonally and then into a kite shape.

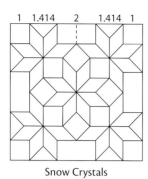

Snow Crystals

Looking at the outside edge of the block, you see a square in the corner, which gets a value of 1. We know the long side of the triangle is 1.414, but what about the rectangle in the center? The rectangle is made from two diamonds coming together at the point. The side of the triangle is equal to the side of the square, so the rectangle would get a value of 2.

$$1 + 1.414 + 2 + 1.414 + 1 = 6.828$$

It is doubtful you would want to attempt this block in anything smaller than 12″ right now, so let's start there.

$$12″ ÷ 6.828 = 1.76″$$

This means the sides of the squares, the triangles, and the diamonds are 1¾″ finished. The rectangle would be 1¾″ × 3½″ finished.

> *tip* Cut a 3¾″ square into quarters diagonally to get triangles with the straight grain on the long edge. (Do you remember how we came up with this measurement? The side of the triangle is 1.75″. 1.75″ × 1.414 = 2.47″—round up to 2.5″. This is the finished size. 2.5″ + 1.25″ [seam allowance for quarter-square triangles] = 3.75″ cut).

What would be the template size for a 15½″ block? And why would you make it 15½″ instead of 15″?

$$15″ ÷ 6.83 = 2.19″$$

This is not a ruler-friendly number. You are close to working in ¹⁄₁₆″ numbers— need we say more?

$$15.5″ ÷ 6.83 = 2.27″, \text{ or } 2¼″ \qquad \text{This is a much friendlier number.}$$

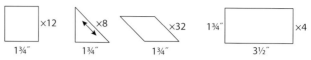

Template sizes needed (finished measurements)

You will start to see that these blocks are not the standard sizes we have been working with in previous volumes. This is one of the reasons these blocks stand alone in most of the quilts in which they are used.

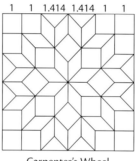

Carpenter's Wheel

This block might give you cold chills to think about piecing right now, but the drafting is straightforward. Reading along the top edge of the block, you can see there are four squares and two triangles.

$$1 + 1 + 1.414 + 1.414 + 1 + 1 = 6.828$$

This is the same as the Snow Crystals block. Obviously, the formula will give the same answers as above.

$$12″ ÷ 6.828 = 1.76″$$

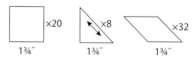

Template sizes needed
(finished measurements)

A 12″ block will use 1¾″ templates.

What other size blocks can you make with ruler-friendly numbers? Here is a chart of decimal equivalents to help with the calculator answers.

Metric conversions / Decimal equivalents

Metric	Decimal
0.03125	¹⁄₃₂
0.0625	¹⁄₁₆
0.09375	³⁄₃₂
0.1	¹⁄₁₀
0.125	⅛
0.14286	⅐
0.15625	⁵⁄₃₂
0.16667	⅙
0.1875	³⁄₁₆
0.2	⅕
0.21875	⁷⁄₃₂
0.25	¼
0.28571	²⁄₇
0.3	³⁄₁₀
0.28125	⁹⁄₃₂
0.3125	⁵⁄₁₆
0.33333	⅓
0.34375	¹¹⁄₃₂
0.375	⅜
0.4	⅖
0.40625	¹³⁄₃₂
0.42857	³⁄₇
0.4375	⁷⁄₁₆
0.46875	¹⁵⁄₃₂
0.5	½
0.53125	¹⁷⁄₃₂

Metric	Decimal
0.5625	⁹⁄₁₆
0.57143	⁴⁄₇
0.59375	¹⁹⁄₃₂
0.6	⅗
0.625	⅝
0.65625	²¹⁄₃₂
0.66667	⅔
0.6875	¹¹⁄₁₆
0.7	⁷⁄₁₀
0.71429	⁵⁄₇
0.71875	²³⁄₃₂
0.75	¾
0.78125	²⁵⁄₃₂
0.8	⅘
0.8125	¹³⁄₁₆
0.83333	⅚
0.84375	²⁷⁄₃₂
0.85714	⁶⁄₇
0.875	⅞
0.9	⁹⁄₁₀
0.90625	²⁹⁄₃₂
0.9375	¹⁵⁄₁₆
0.96875	³¹⁄₃₂

Ready for another one? Let's move on to stars that are octagons placed inside of a square—Rolling Stars.

Look at the illustration. This block can be a bit of a puzzle until you realize that the eight-pointed star actually "fits" into a square that is on point inside the larger total block.

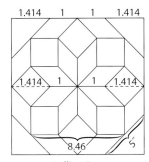

Rolling Star

The first thing you need to do is find the side of this internal square. Begin by dividing the side of the outer square in half, and then multiplying that number by 1.414. This answer is the length of the side of the internal square. Divide that number by 3.414 and you will know the size of the square and the diamond. Work with a 12″ block again.

12″ ÷ 2 = 6″ × 1.414 = 8.48″ ÷ 3.414 = 2.49″ = 2½″

To find the size of the corner triangles, add the length of the side of the diamond twice.

2.5″ + 2.5″ = 5″

Subtract this number from the size of the block and divide by 2, because there are two triangles.

12″ − 5″ = 7″ ÷ 2 = 3½″

Therefore, you will need 2½″ squares, 2½″ diamonds (strips and segments cut 2¼″ wide), and 3½″ triangles (two 4⅜″ squares cut diagonally).

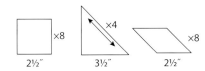

Template sizes needed (finished measurement)

There are times that it is not necessary to do a lot of math, as the internal units are subdivisions of a basic block. St. Louis Star is one of these blocks. If you look at it closely, you will see that it is a simple LeMoyne Star, but each point has been divided in half point to point. If you look even closer, you will see there is another division that gives an ice-cream cone shape between the points. This shape is developed by connecting the points straight across from one another with lines just in the left and right sides of the square that is the center of the block. By connecting these lines across from each pair of points, you get the internal division. You will have four different template shapes instead of three as in the LeMoyne Star.

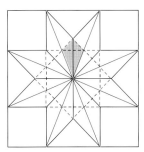

St. Louis Star created by subdividing LeMoyne Star

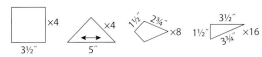

Template sizes needed for 12″ block

Can you take these blocks and work through the measurements using the formulas to double-check our numbers? Now is a good time to test your new knowledge. You might want to test yourself by choosing a different size block and reworking the math to come up with the correct answers for the new size. If you are ever unsure about your answers, draft the block on graph paper and measure the units physically. This is also a good way for you to combine the mental and the visual elements at the same time.

As you analyze more blocks, you are apt to see many basic blocks with many subdivisions, which will in turn make it easier to understand how they are pieced together.

Job well done! If you don't completely understand all this yet, keep working at it. Those two magic numbers—3.414 and 1.414—are all you need. Just learn to look at the divisions in the blocks. This makes grids and nine-patches a walk in the park! That is why you are now a senior.

Now let's put all this effort to work and learn to construct the blocks. We will be using all the measurements given above. If you need to make templates, do so before we start. If you have a collection of precut templates, such as the Perfect Patchwork Templates, go through them and pull out the shapes you need. If you don't have the right size, you might want to challenge yourself to redraft the block to use the sizes you have. These are just samples, so it doesn't matter what size block you make. If you think 12″ will be too tedious and difficult, redraft the blocks to a larger size. Good practice for your math skills!

LESSON FOUR:
Construction techniques for complex blocks

We will give you the highlights for making these blocks but not step-by-step instructions or templates and patterns. We trust that you have made the samples in Class 440 and are very familiar with the concepts of Y-seams and set-in piecing. If not, go back and master the simple LeMoyne Star before you go any further. All blocks are 12″, unless the block is very complex. We also want you to understand the drafting and how to determine what sizes to cut the pieces by mastering Lessons Two and Three. As you scan through these blocks, you will realize that if you keep them all 12″ square, some of the pieces will be very small and perhaps difficult for you to handle. Feel free to draft these patterns to any size of your choosing. We want you to learn the processes involved, not stress over tiny pieces. As you gain experience working with set-in piecing, you will find small pieces easier to work with; but for now,

keep it to your comfort level. We do not include templates, as one of the purposes of this class is to make sure you understand drafting. You get a total understanding of the inner workings of the pieces of each block once you have worked them out by drafting them. There are times when you will need a template, and what better way to get one than by drafting your own!

Here is a list of tips that we think will help you to be successful.

✻ **Cutting accurately is of utmost importance.** If the angles or sizes are off by even a couple of threads, the points won't be as sharp as needed once sewn.

✻ **Make a sample block first.** We have found that the first time making a new pattern can be pretty confusing. The diagrams are helpful, but you still have to work out how to do the pressing as well as which seams are sewn edge to edge and which ones are sewn just to the seamline (dot). This might sound like a lot of extra work, but you will not have to use the seam ripper nearly as often if you do it.

✻ **Speaking of seam rippers, invest in the best one you can find.** You want a seam ripper with a very thin and narrow blade. Many of the seam rippers on the market are thick and bulky, making it hard to get under the stitches. When sewing over many layers while matching points, the stitches can get very short. If you have to take them out, you will really appreciate a good ripper.

✻ **If you are rotary cutting all of your pieces, make sure to take the time to go back to trim the corners and points.** The Perfect Patchwork Templates corner system gives you the great advantage of getting the placement of the units right before sewing.

✻ **Go through the layout illustrations and study the intersections that need you to stop sewing at the seamline.** Many of the blocks do not need dots marked on all the corners and points, just the ones that need to have a piece set into them.

✻ **You might find it helpful to cut the outside edge pieces a bit larger than called for.** It is so important to be able to join this edge to another block later on, but if the edges are not straight, this is tricky. If the pieces are cut larger, they can be squared and trimmed to exactly ¼″ from the points once the block is completed.

✻ **As you join each piece to another and press, check that points are ¼″ from the edge.** If not, you will usually find that the edges were not aligned exactly, or the seam was not sewn straight. Often the pressing is the problem.

Now is the time to analyze what is causing the problem and correct it. When you have six to eight points coming together at one spot, any inaccuracies will prevent you from having impressive points.

※ **For the sharpest points, sew off the edge each time you add a piece to the point.** This gives you a sharp point to aim for when matching with other points. Sewing dot to dot on these points is too unstable for matching.

※ **When cutting, pay close attention to grainline placement for each shape.** Avoid having bias on any outside edge of the block.

Keeping all this in mind, let's start making stars! We will walk you through the first few blocks, then let you start to think through the system and apply the techniques you are learning as you continue.

Drafted size to rotary cut size/shape

Drafted size	Rotary cut size
☐ 1¾″	2¼″ cut
☐ 2½″	3″ cut
☐ 3½″	4″ cut
◺ 2½″ / 1¾″	⊠ 3¾″ or ▢ 2⅝″
◺ 5″ / 3½″	⊠ 6¼″ or ▢ 4⅜″
▱ 1¼″	1⅜″ cut strip, segment cut 1⅜″
▱ 1¾″	1¾″ cut strip, segment cut 1¾″
▱ 2½″	2¼″ cut strip, segment cut 2¼″

12″ Striped Star

This star is constructed exactly the same as the LeMoyne Star, except the diamond points are constructed of two long strips of fabric.

If you have not worked through the math and drafting outlined in Class 440 and here in Class 450, we will give you a brief overview. This is the easiest star of this section and if you do not understand where the numbers are coming from, you can get very lost in the math. So, go back now and work through the formulas in Class 440 and the preceding lessons in this class so you understand the math from this point forward.

Using the formula from Method Three, Class 440, Lesson One (page 51), we know that the finished size of the diamond is 3½″. Following through, then:

$$3.5″ ÷ 1.414 = 2.47″ \sim 2.5″$$

This is the flat side–to–flat side measurement of the diamond. To determine the width of each strip:

$$2.5″ ÷ 2 \text{ (\# of strips in diamond)} =$$
$$1.25″ + 0.5″ \text{ (seam allowance)} = 1.75″$$

Therefore, you will need to cut two strips of the fabric of your choice 1¾″ wide by the width of the fabric. Sew these strips together, press, and trim. Using your 4″ diamond

template (seam allowances included), cut eight diamonds. If you are using a straight ruler, start with an exact 45° angle cut. Measure down the strip 4″ and cut your first diamond. To check for accuracy, fold the diamond in half. The middle corners should line up exactly. Continue until you have eight diamonds.

Once all of the pieces are cut, construct the same as the LeMoyne Star.

Star of the East

This star is in the same family as Striped Star, only the seam is point to point instead of side to side. You will once again be sewing two strips together, but this time cut 2″ wide. You will need two strip sets. We suggest that you press this seam open. Draw a line point to point on the top of your template. This line will be placed directly on top of the seam before cutting. Cut eight diamonds.

Because of the position of the template on the strip set, all the edges are now bias, so be very gentle when you handle these diamonds. When making the first sub-units of two diamonds and the triangle, carefully align the outside edges. This point of intersection is just as important as the center of the star. Once the triangle is attached to two diamonds and pressed, fold right sides together, place very fine pins in the seams of the two diamonds, and align the seams exactly. Pin the length of the seam and be sure to pin at the point. Stitch from the triangle to the points. Once the seam is sewn, open it and check the center. The seams need to intersect exactly here. You have twice as many points coming together in this star, and if one is off, they will all be off. Take your time and make any corrections necessary as you go. Press this seam open.

Once the squares are attached to the above units, check the outside edge where the points are. The center seam of the diamond should be exactly at the intersection of all the pieces. We are looking for accurate, sharp points.

Formosa Tea Leaf

Four of the diamonds in Formosa Tea Leaf are pieced; the other four are plain diamonds. Color the points to your liking. You will need a visual aid when piecing the small units together. The pieced points are built similarly to a Log Cabin block. You may want to draft this block on graph paper if you are unsure of the sizes of the units and where the measurement came from.

The small diamonds in the points are 1⅛″ finished (⅞″ from flat side to flat side) for a 12″ block. You can either

rotary cut the diamonds or use #36 of Set E if you have Perfect Patchwork Templates. Cut strips 1⅜″ wide, establish a 45° angle at the end of the strip, and measure down from the cut 1⅜″. For our sample, we cut eight blue and four red diamonds this size.

Pieced diamond breakout

The remaining three pieces are parallelograms and are the same size, but with one color change. The rotary-cut size for this unit is shown in the illustration below. You will need to cut a 1⅜″ strip of each fabric.

Starting with the red fabric and following the diagram below, establish a 45° angle at the end of the strip. Be sure you cut the same angle as shown. Measure down the strip 2⅛″ and make a 45° angle cut. Cut four of these units. *If you are cutting layers, make sure all the strip pieces are right side up.* If the strips are folded in half, you will get one and one reverse.

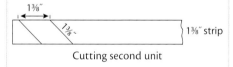
Cutting second unit

Look closely at the way this piece is positioned in the diamond. You have a blue diamond and a red diamond joined together first. Press this seam open. On the left side of this unit, add one of the red parallelograms you just cut. Carefully align the edges and the offset pointed ends. Press the seams open. Make four units.

Combining diamonds and parallelogram

The next round of color is background. Notice that there is one and

one reverse of this parallelogram. Cut these double using a strip folded in half. This will give you one of each per cut. Make four cuts, each 2⅛″ long.

Add one of the parallelograms to the right side of the constructed unit. Be sure that the angles are in the correct position and the offset points at each end are positioned for your seam allowance. Repeat for all four units. Press the seams open.

Attaching cream parallelogram

The mirror-image parallelogram will be attached to the remaining blue diamond. Once these units are combined and seams pressed open, add this unit to the left side of the previously constructed pieces. This is the first time we have addressed matching the seams on a 45° angle. There isn't a slick trick like there was for 60° diamonds. This time pinning will be necessary.

Adding last side

The match is ¼″ in from the raw edge. Align the edges and get the points into the correct alignment. At the seam that needs to match, insert a pin from the wrong side of the top segment, directly in the seamline and ¼″ from the edge. Push the pin into the right side of the underneath segment, directly in the seamline and ¼″ from the edge. Do not take the pin stitch yet. Hold the pin straight up and down through both points.

Hold the seam allowances together between your thumb and finger to keep both seamlines matched. Turn the pin and bring the point of the pin up through the fabric following the underneath seamline. If you look closely at the raw edge, you should see a ⅛″ gap between the ends of the two seams. When you get used to looking for this gap, you might find you no longer need to pin.

Now that the diamond is constructed, place your 4″ diamond template on top and check for accuracy. If there is any problem that requires trimming, make sure you keep the template lined up exactly with the small blue diamond that goes in the center of the block for consistency. Trim to the exact size of the template.

Cut four red 4″ diamonds, four 4″ squares, and four 4″ half-square triangles of background fabric. You are now ready to construct the star in the same manner as the LeMoyne Star.

Dove in the Window

Now that you have made a Formosa Tea Leaf block, does this Dove in the Window star look familiar?

When you analyze the points, you will see that there are two different-colored doves with a simpler block in between them. When you look at those blocks, you see there are two with one color placement and two that are mirror images to those.

Therefore, you have four different points in this design.

Four different points

You have the choice of piecing the side units using a diamond template or strip piecing.

If strip piecing, the strip width is cut 1⅜″. There are four strip sets needed—two sets are made of three strips joined, using cream-blue-cream and cream-brown-cream; the other two strip sets are made of two strips joined, using brown-cream and blue-cream. You will need about 9″ of length for each and will cut four segments from each.

Construct a strip set using one each of blue and cream and another strip set of brown and cream. Press the seams open. Using a ruler, establish the first 45° angle cut. Measure down the length of the strip set 1⅜″ and cut the first segment. Remember to keep the ruler lines straight with the internal seams of the strip set. Continue cutting until you have four segments. Repeat with the second strip set.

The second strip set is constructed as you have learned throughout this series—sew two strips together, press the seam open, measure and trim if necessary, and then add the third strip. Press the seam open, and then measure and trim. This strip set has the dark fabric as the middle strip.

To cut the larger diamonds, you will need one strip each of the three colors cut 2⅛″ wide. Cut four cream, two blue, and two brown diamonds.

note This star can also be made using a hexagon instead of an octagon. It is called Blue Birds when in this configuration.

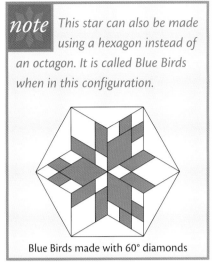
Blue Birds made with 60° diamonds

The construction is very similar to that of Formosa Tea Leaf. The segments are sewn to alternating sides of the larger diamond as shown.

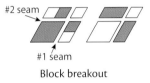
#2 seam
#1 seam
Block breakout

St. Louis Star

St. Louis Star progresses in difficulty from Striped Star and Star of the East. You no longer have eight diamonds. Instead, you have eight ice-cream cone–shaped pieces in the center and eight narrow points that are offset from the center cones.

This block will require you to draft the pattern onto a 12″ square of graph paper to get the template shapes needed for the ice-cream cones and the sharp points. Once drafted, carefully cut out the graph paper right on the line. Glue these shapes onto extra-thick template plastic (see Resources, page 128). Mark a dot in the outside corners of the cones and the inside corners of the star points.

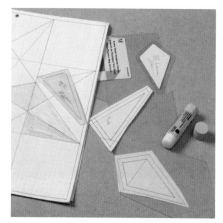

Preparing templates

When cutting the star points, the template will be used right side up *and* wrong side up, as it is a mirror image in the block. When cutting, do not fold the fabric into fourths. Cut the fabric a bit larger than the template and then stack layers of it right side up. Cut four star prints at a time. You will need eight of each color. Mark the seamline dot at the center seam and the corners that fit into the cones.

Begin by sewing the cones together, working with the pieces as if they were the inside of a star. Begin at the seamline dot at the outside edges of the cones and sew off the edges at the center point. Sew pairs together first and press well. Add two pairs together so you have two halves of the block. Join this seam and try to get all the points exactly in the center of the block. Stitch dot to dot. Press all seams the same direction, but press the center seam open.

Sew the two halves of the star points together, stitching to the seamline dot on the edge that will connect with the cones and stitching off the edge at the outside point. Press the seams open.

Carefully set the point seam into the cone. To begin, align the left side of the point with the point of the cone. Pin in place to keep it square; also pin the point seam allowance back out of the way.

Stitch from the dot at the outside edge to the stitching. We preferred to turn the piece over and work from the cone side. It is easier to see the stitching as you come up to it.

Once stitched, slide the point over to the opposite side of the cone and repeat. Remove the pins and check the front. You are looking for the long seam to intersect exactly to make a straight line through the entire point. Continue around the center, repeating this process. We sewed in every other point first and then added the remaining points. Be sure you don't catch any seam allowances in the stitching. Press seams toward the cones.

Now you are ready to set in the corners and the side triangles. Check that the star is lying flat in each step of the process. This is the point of construction where if things are not square and straight, the block will be out of shape and anything *but* flat. If you drafted the pattern on graph paper, lay the pieces on top of the paper as you complete each step to check for accuracy.

This block takes time and concentration to make sure that all the seams end at the same dot and all edges are aligned accurately as you go. You may

have to remove some stitches here and there to realign something, but you will be very proud of yourself when you get it finished.

Rolling Star

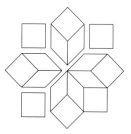

Block breakout

As you can see from the breakout, Rolling Star is not much more difficult than a basic LeMoyne Star, but accuracy is a must. To begin, lay out the pieces to create the basic Y-seam units. In this block, it is diamonds to squares instead of triangles. Stitch the square onto the left diamond, sewing off the edge. Press toward the diamond. Add the right diamond, sewing up to the stitching. Press toward the diamond. Close the diamond seam. You will have four units joined when finished.

Center units

Join two of these units together by sewing the diamond seams, stopping at the seamline dots at the outside points. Set in the square, sewing just to the previous stitching on each side. Make two of these units.

Joining two units

Join these units through the center, bringing all eight points together. Stitch only to the seamline (dot) on the outside edge. Once the center is constructed, set in the remaining squares. We have found that if the last seam of the square is sewn off the raw edge, it is easier to get the points sharp and accurate when adding the outside diamonds.

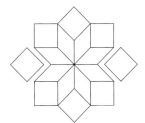

Center complete

Start adding the diamonds around the outside edge. Turn the block from back to front if necessary to see where you are going.

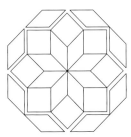

Adding diamonds

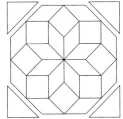

Finishing with corner triangles

The final step is to add the outside corner triangles. That wasn't so bad, so let's build on it and try Snow Crystals.

Snow Crystals

Snow Crystals is an expansion of Rolling Star. The center unit is the same (but smaller), but there are corners made of half eight-pointed stars and rectangles set in on the sides.

Block breakout

Begin by constructing the corner sections. These are just like LeMoyne Stars, so approach them the same way. Sew the diamonds to the triangles and then add the corner squares. Make four of these.

Construct the center the same as you did for Rolling Star. Stop once the diamonds are set in around the center.

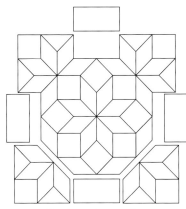

Putting units together

When attaching the corner units to the center, treat them as if you were putting together the center of a LeMoyne Star. You have seven points coming together, so baste the center of each to check for alignment. Set in the rectangles last, starting with the long side. Close the short sides of the rectangle last.

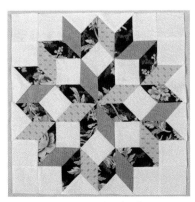

Carpenter's Wheel

The order in which we are putting Carpenter's Wheel together is taught by Sharyn Craig. You will find other breakouts, but Sharyn's offers the fewest stops and starts when putting the four units together. If you look at the block closely, you will see that there are four corners and two center units to construct.

We strongly suggest that you make a mock-up of the block color to keep the pieces in the proper place. Because of the way this block is broken up during construction, it is easy to get the wrong color diamonds in a position, not realizing it until you are ready to assemble the units. Does it sound like we know this from experience?

You will start by making four of the center unit. These are made up of two diamonds added to a square, and then two more diamonds added to the opposite sides. Press seams toward the diamonds. Check the points on the side seams—they need to be exactly ¼″ from the edge.

Center unit

Next is the construction of the four corners. Does this remind you of Tumbling Blocks? The construction is similar. The dots indicate the seams that need to be sewn to the dots.

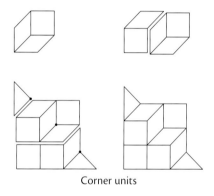

Corner units

The center units are next, added to two of the corner units.

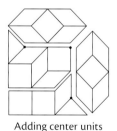

Adding center units

You now have four units. The first seam will be joining the two top units together. Pin carefully when you sew the long part of the seam, as you have six points coming together in the center of the seam.

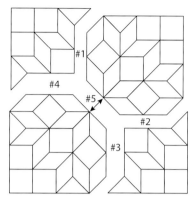

Putting components together

The lower right corner is added next, followed by the seam joining the top left and bottom left corners. As with the LeMoyne Star, the center seam is last.

LESSON FIVE:

Lone Stars

We don't know if there is a specific grouping for the blocks we are going to play with here, but they all have the same thing in common—diamond points containing many more diamond points. Whether each point has four small diamonds or the entire quilt is one big star with dozens of small diamonds in each point, they all have a similar look. Because there are so many things we can do with them, we didn't think one block would do this design justice. We will start with the following illustrated basic 12″ blocks to work through the design. Then you will have a chance to play with larger Lone Star blocks, where color placement and accents really get to show off. There are several illustrations to start you thinking about color placement in the star points. You will find this a limitless process, as there are endless ways to color in the small diamonds, and they can be any size and quantity you want.

Morning Star

Blazing Star

Virginia Star

DRAFTING LONE STARS

Drafting for any star of this type can be simply done using the Virginia and Blazing Star designs. They are all related. Let's learn to draft them so that we can make them any size you need for your own designs. These should seem easy after the mind-benders you just finished.

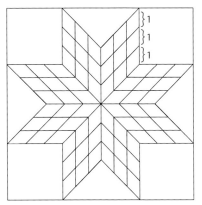

Virginia Star

The goal is to find the size of the small diamonds that subdivide the larger diamond. Start by determining the size of the finished block and finding the basic measurements.

We will use a 12″ block again.

$$12″ ÷ 3.414 = 3.5″$$

As you probably know by heart now, that is the size of the side of the square, diamond, and triangle. The next step is to know how many divisions you want within the diamond. Virginia Star has three.

$$3.5″ ÷ 3 = 1.166″ = 1⅙″$$

This would be the size of your small diamonds.

Template sizes needed

> **tip** Cut a 6¼″ square into quarters diagonally to get the large triangles with the straight grain on the long edge.

Blazing Star and Morning Star are similar to Virginia Star, except they have only two divisions in the points. The size of the small diamonds within the points is the same for both Morning Star and Blazing Star. Blazing Star has two divisions in the corner and side units that need additional measurements, so we will work through Blazing Star, knowing that the measurements we find will fit the needs of Morning Star for the diamonds.

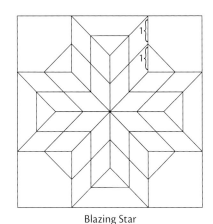

Blazing Star

$$12″ ÷ 3.414 = 3.5″ ÷ 2 = 1.75″, or 1¾″$$

This is the side measurement for the small diamonds. This also tells you the short sides of the trapezoid in the corner.

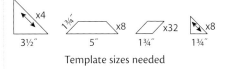

Template sizes needed

DESIGNING WITH MULTIPLE POINTS

We want to introduce you to how versatile the design is. The difference between Morning Star and Blazing Star is the addition of a small triangle in the corner square and side triangle, giving a more dimensional and octagonal look to the block. Virginia Star is a miniature Lone Star. If you decide to make a full-size quilt with this pattern, we suggest you purchase one of the many excellent books on the market that deal only with Lone Stars. Books by Jan Krentz are very inspirational, but we think the very best book on this star was written by Judy Martin in 1987—*Shining Star Quilts* (ISBN 0-943721-00-8). Judy delves into all the variations of the basic Lone Star in depth, as well as borders and quilting ideas.

To the right you will see that the placement of color can totally change the visual dimension of the block when different formulas are used. There are three blank blocks below for you to photocopy and play with to create your own ideas. Have fun!

Most common color placement— concentric rings of color radiate from center.

Every second ring is white to make checkerboards.

Alternating star points— star points are colored two different ways.

Color chains—colors are placed lengthwise instead of concentrically.

Color bands—colors are in rings, but one color is flanked on both sides by same color.

Center diamond of each point has strong, contrasting accent color.

Worksheets

When the block is expanded and becomes the entire quilt top, color placement can be subtle or dramatic.

Checkerboard layout—appliqué in triangle and square units would be lovely on this quilt.

Using smaller diamonds within two concentric rings

Kalimantan, designed by Jinny Beyer

We certainly hope you are inspired to learn to make these blocks after playing with them and seeing their potential!

Now it is time to go through the processes, tips, and tricks for constructing each one of them. When piecing Morning Star and Blazing Star, you can use either templates or strip sets. This decision depends on the quantity of blocks you are making. If you choose scrappy colors within the points, templates would be the most time efficient. If all the colors are repeated the same way in each star point, strip sets would save a lot of time. We suggest that you try both methods and see which gives you the most success. Once you learn to piece Virginia Star, the same method of strip piecing will allow you to make a Lone Star any size you want. It is along the same design idea as the 60° stars you learned in Class 430.

Let's start with the simplest block, Morning Star. If you are working with templates, you know from the drafting unit that you will need to cut 4″ corner squares, 4″ triangles (6¼″ square cut in half diagonally twice), and 32 – 1¾″ diamonds. Remember that these are the cut measurements.

If you are going to strip piece the small diamonds, you will need to cut 1¾″-wide strips, each about 18″ long. Sew them in pairs as diagrammed on your color plan or mock-up.

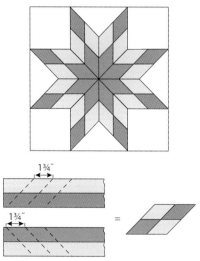

Color plan and corresponding strip sets

Once the strip sets are sewn and the seams are pressed open, establish a 45° angle at the left end of each strip, paying close attention to the change in direction of the angle of one strip set to the other. Cut eight 1¾″ diamonds from each strip set. Keep an eye on the alignment of the ruler with the cut edge and the seam. You may have to realign the angled edge once in a while, depending on how straight you sewed and pressed. Double- and triple-check that each diamond is exactly 45° both ways, as well as 1¾″ in both directions.

We are going to review the process of matching 45° seams here, as it may have gotten lost in all the drafting and piecing you have been doing. Unlike 60° diamonds, the seam allowances do not match up to one another for easy and accurate placement. Each intersecting seam needs to be positioned and pinned, and the more intersections there are, the more pinning is necessary.

Each point of the Morning Star is essentially a four-patch, and the segments will pair together the same way, though at an angle. To start the intersection-matching process, there are a couple of things to visually check. This is a rather difficult angle to match because the segments angle away from each other. At the beginning of the seam, there will be a ½″ offset between the point of the underneath segment and the corner of the top segment.

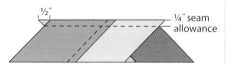

Seam allowance alignment

If you can visually line up the edges using the ½″ spacing, your seams stand a great chance of matching. Until you can gauge this distance by eye, you will have to consistently pin each seam intersection. Treat these strips very carefully, as the edges you are sewing are bias and can easily stretch out of shape.

To align and pin a seam intersection, stick a pin straight down through the fabric at the first seam. If you can't visually gauge ¼″ in from the raw edge for the seam, measure and make a tiny mark. If this width is too wide or too narrow, the points will not come together. Push the pin through the second layer (underneath), ¼″ from the edge and exactly in the seam.

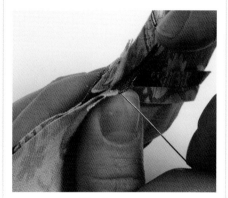

Pin placement

There are two schools of thought about how to pin from here. Some leave this pin vertical, adding a pin just to the left of the vertical pin. The thought is that the seam is less likely to shift as you sew toward a pin before the intersection. The second thought is to position the pin vertically and then hold onto the edge securely, turn the pin, and bring the point of the pin up through the fabric following the underneath seamline. The concept is that the pin holds more accurately when it is on the straight grain.

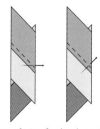

Position of pins for both techniques

Remove the pins as you come to them if your machine can't sew over them. We find that the extra-fine Clover Patchwork Pins are perfect for this, as most machines don't have a problem going over them.

If you really study what these angles are doing as you sew them, you will see that there is a ⅛″ gap between the seamline of the bottom segment and the raw edge of the left seam allowance of the top segment. Another visual aid is the points extending beyond the seam allowance at the intersection. If you notice that they are not the same height, then the seams are not properly aligned.

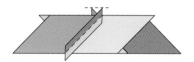

Look for point height beyond raw edge.

Left: seam allowance too narrow
Center: seam allowance too wide
Right: proper seam allowance

Once the seam is finished and you have accurate intersections, it is a good idea to check for accuracy of the completed diamond. Draw a 4″ diamond onto freezer paper with permanent marker and iron it onto your ironing board. Once the four-patch diamonds are pressed, compare them with the paper pattern. If they are out of shape, pin through the paper and ironing board cover to press. Use only glass-head pins when doing this, keeping the heads beyond the outside edge of the diamond. Press with a bit of steam to block the unit to correct any distortion.

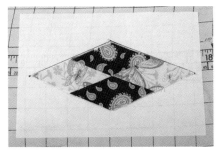

Correcting any distortion by blocking

If you are working with templates, you can place the appropriate-sized template on top of the unit to check for size and alignment.

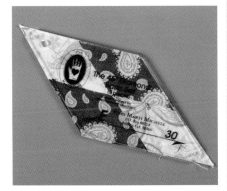

Checking for accuracy with template

Virginia Star

We are going to first work through Virginia Star and then finish with a larger Lone Star. Virginia Star is made of nine-patch diamonds. This is just an additional strip added to the strip sets of Morning Star. Virginia Star, however, does not always work out in a ruler-friendly way. For example, so far we have been making 12″ sample blocks for this lesson, but when you

try to divide the Virginia Star into a 12″ block, you get some not-nice numbers:

$$3\tfrac{1}{2}''\ \text{diamond} \div 1.414 = 2.47''\ \text{or}\ 2.5''$$

That's all fine until you divide 2.5″ by 3 and you get 0.833″. If you round down you to 0.75″, there is a 0.08″ difference, and over the course of three strips, your diamond points will end up ¼″ smaller than needed. If you round up to 0.875″, you have a 0.04″ difference, making the diamond points ⅛″ larger than desired. Neither situation is ideal, but to make the block close to 12″, we chose to round the finished size strips in the diamond up to ⅞″ (1⅜″ cut). This made our block measure nearly 13″ square. Virginia Star is a classic example of what we talked about earlier with Carpenter's Wheel. Picking a 15″ block doesn't work out for Carpenter's Wheel, but 15½″ does. Same with Virginia Star—you will need to work the formula until you find a size that is ruler friendly. When you use the most ruler-friendly measurements, you end up with an odd-sized star. A solution to this problem is to use only Virginia Star blocks in your quilt. Trying to draft an alternate block to an odd size may be beyond doable.

With that said, we chose to use ruler-friendly measurements to make an odd-sized star. The strips are cut 1⅜″ wide and 20″ long. Plan your color positions in the block by coloring a mock-up. This will show you the order of the colors for each strip set. We suggest that you number the small diamonds and identify the rows by A, B, and C as shown.

Virginia Star point breakout

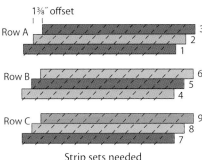

Strip sets needed

When sewing the strips together, offset the ends by 1⅜″. Press seam allowances open. Trim the left end of each strip set at a 45° angle. Double-check that the 45° ruler line is straight against the raw edge of the strip set, or work with a triangle ruler as we did with the 60° diamond stars. The triangle ruler has lines that will align with your seams, helping you to make sure that the angle is positioned exactly. If you have problems with accurate cutting, this is, by far, the most accurate way to cut these angles (refer back to Class 420, Lesson One, page 21).

Cut eight segments from each strip set. Keep them in a stack as you cut. You can chainstitch these segments together, joining Row A and Row B first, checking for point intersection accuracy, and then pressing the seam open. This is also a good time to check that the 45° angle is holding true after sewing. Add Row C next. Once this seam is pressed, block the diamond if necessary to make it accurate.

Once all eight points are assembled, we are back to the basic construction of a LeMoyne Star, only this time with even more seam intersections to match.

If you want to combine several of these stars together into a quilt, follow the diagram for layout. You would not finish each star into a block for this setting.

Joining stars to make row

The pieces needed to join the stars are 3¾″ triangles (6⅝″ squares cut in half diagonally in both directions), 3¾″ squares (4¼″ cut), 7½″ squares (8″ cut), and 7½″ × 3¾″ rectangles (8″ × 4¼″ cut). If you are at all unsure how we got these measurements, please go back and review the drafting. If you know the size of the square and you know the size of the side of the diamond, this should be easy for you to figure out.

Join the stars in a horizontal row by adding a triangle at each end and the small square between each pair of stars. Remember to mark the seamlines and sew dot to dot when constructing. Make as many rows as your design calls for.

When joining the rows, you will need to connect them using the small and large squares, as well as the rectangles on the ends.

Joining rows

Finish the edges by setting the squares into the corners and the triangles and rectangles along the sides.

tip If you want to make larger stars to fill more space with less work, you could make 18″ stars.

Lone Star pillow

For this size block, cut:

- star point strips 1½″ wide

- corner squares 5¾″

- side triangles from a 9⅜″ square, cut diagonally in both directions

Do you trust our measurements? We have been known to make a mistake or two in this series of books, so we strongly suggest that you do the calculator math and double-check us, as we did not make this block to test the measurements. If you think 18″ is rather large, how about 15″? You pick and do the math, and you will have your own pattern.

LESSON SIX:
The quilts
PROJECT ONE: *STARS APLENTY*

Stars Aplenty

Quilt top size: 46″ × 46″

Yardage needed:

2½ yards cream background (includes yardage for the border)

¼ yard brown paisley

⅛ yard each of 4 teals, 3 greens, and 1 brown to coordinate with brown paisley

This quilt is a remake of a quilt Sharyn Craig made for *The Art of Classic Quiltmaking,* but with a few changes. From the block patterns given earlier in this class, pick four of your favorite blocks and make them 12″ finished in coordinating colors. You will notice that two of the blocks in Carrie's quilt are not quite like those covered at the beginning of this class. The first is actually called Liberty Star and is made up of three strips instead of the two used in Striped Star. The other is a variation of Star of the East, or Divided Star (as a joke Carrie called hers Partially Divided Star). Both of these variations are easy enough for you to figure out if you want to make your quilt like Carrie's.

Liberty Star

Partially Divided Star

Make nine 6″ LeMoyne Stars, mixing up the colors you have chosen to work with for this quilt.

Once you have both sizes of the star blocks completed, it is time to set the blocks together.

Complete quilt layout

To create the center block with the small LeMoyne Star in the middle, you will need to add corner triangles to the small block, just like you would to the corners of a quilt set on point. Cut two 10″ squares of background fabric and cut in half diagonally. Attach two of the triangles to two opposite sides of the star block. Press and trim the points flush with the other two sides of the block. Add the remaining two triangles to the other sides. Once this large block is pressed and starched, you can trim it down to measure exactly 12½″.

For the side-setting triangles incorporating the 6″ LeMoyne Stars at the point, refer back to the instructions for making *Cabin in the Cotton* in Volume 2, Class 240 (pages 47 and 48). The size of the blocks is different, but the technique is identical to the one used for making the side-setting triangles for that quilt. Follow those instructions.

Next, add the corner triangles to make your quilt top square. Remember how to do this? Take the size of the block and add 2″–3″. Cut a square that size and then cut it in half diagonally.

Finally, to finish the quilt, you will need to cut four 6½″ strips of the fabric you have chosen for your border. Measure your quilt to get the length needed to cut your borders. Sew the two side borders on first, and then add the four LeMoyne Star blocks to the top and bottom border strips. Sew on the top and bottom borders.

PROJECT TWO: HARRIET'S TREADLE ARTS 2009 *SHOP HOP QUILT*

Shop Hop Quilt

Quilt top size: 80″ × 80″

Yardages needed:

For the blocks:

1 yard cream background

¼ yard each of 6–7 different fabrics that coordinate with print fabric listed below

For the quilt top:

2⅔ yards print

1½ yards green

1¼ yards burgundy

1 yard cream

Start by making the eight blocks presented in Lesson Four before assembling the quilt top. The only way this quilt goes together successfully is if all your blocks are the same size. All these blocks need to measure exactly 12½″ square, unfinished.

Once the blocks are finished, cut all the diamonds for both the center and outer rings of the star points. You will rotary cut the diamonds from strips, so you will need a 12″ square ruler to cut the following strips:

❋ 6 – 8⅞″ strips of print

❋ 6 – 8⅞″ strips of green

❋ 4 – 8⅞″ strips of burgundy

Once you have these strips cut, place the 45° line of a 6″ × 24″ ruler along a cut edge. Align the ruler from one corner to establish the 45° angle at one end of the strip. You will get two diamonds from each strip.

Next, using your 12″ square, align the 45° line or center of your square with the same edge you used when cutting the first 45° cut. Slide the ruler down until the first 45° cut is lined up on the 8⅞″ ruler line. Cut the opposite edge.

From your strips, cut:

- ❋ 12 print diamonds
- ❋ 12 green diamonds
- ❋ 8 burgundy diamonds

Now assemble the center portion of the quilt. Lay out four print and four green diamonds, alternated, and place the blocks in each of the eight voids around the outer edge of the center star. Refer to the illustrations for the center of Rolling Star (page 70) to assemble the center portion of your quilt.

To construct each of the eight partial star sections that are on the outside, cut four 17¾″ squares of the cream and then cut each of those squares diagonally twice so you have four triangles from each square.

Lay out the center of your quilt and then place the remaining diamonds (green-print-green or burgundy-print-burgundy) in three-part star points alternating around the center of your quilt top. Once these are in place, add two triangles to the void area of each three-part star. Follow the illustrations to assemble these five-piece star sections of your quilt. You can stack all eight of the partial stars together and chainsew these sections, or you can sew them individually.

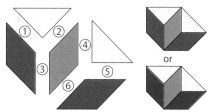

Assembling partial-star sections

Once all eight of the three-part stars are assembled, lay them back out around the center of your quilt top. Follow the numbers in the illustration; these indicate the order in which you need to sew your seams to attach the three-part stars to the center of the quilt.

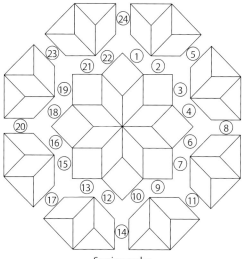

Sewing order

Add the red borders to the four sides that will become the corners of your quilt. Cut four 2″-wide strips. Center each strip with the star points and sew.

Next, cut the large triangles of the print to complete the corners. From the print fabric, cut two 22″ squares and then cut them in half diagonally. Attach these triangles to each of the red strips of the four corners of the quilt to make the quilt square.

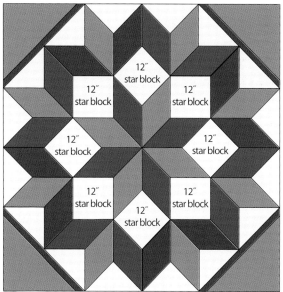

Quilt layout

Class 460

This class is dedicated to Log Cabins in all their various forms. In the past three volumes, we addressed making traditional Log Cabin blocks and setting them in a variety of ways. Now we are going to change things a bit by changing the shape of the center of the Log Cabin to discover how this can take your quilt designs beyond what you thought possible for a simple Log Cabin.

LESSON ONE:

Hexagon Log Cabins

As with Class 410, we are going to address hexagon Log Cabin blocks first. Hexagons are one of the easiest shapes to convert into a Log Cabin block and are extremely easy to piece.

The following illustrations show three Log Cabin quilts made using blocks built around a hexagon. The first quilt, really a table runner, is made by adding the logs to the hexagon in a Courthouse Steps fashion. The logs are added to three of the sides and then pressed and trimmed. Logs are then added to the remaining three sides and pressed and trimmed again. This method is continued until you have the number of rounds around the center that you desire.

The next two quilts have equilateral triangles added to three sides of the hexagon. The color of these small triangles will begin either the light or dark sides of the blocks. The red and blue illustration uses small white triangles, letting the blue and red colors be more prevalent in the quilt. Large white hexagons are bordered on all six sides by red, which is the last round of each block. The large white hexagon is a wonderful place for quilting.

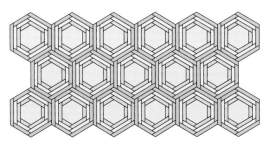

Table runner with large hexagon center

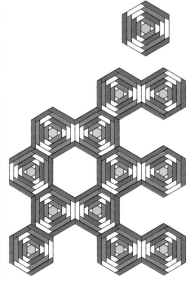

Red and blue hexagon Log Cabin, often called Milky Way

The next quilt shows the opposite coloration. The dark small triangles were added to the red center hexagon, causing the light sides to take precedence. To balance the lack of dark, a large red hexagon was used.

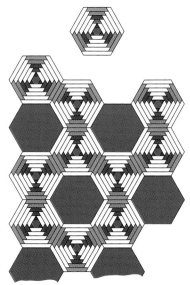

Brown and red hexagon Log Cabin

When blocks do not have straight edges and square corners, the sides of the quilt will not be straight, unless you cut away part of the pieced block. Here is an example of how to handle the ends of the Milky Way quilt previously illustrated.

Edge treatment for large hexagons

What would you get if you used a coloration like that of a square Log Cabin block?

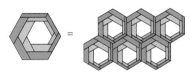

Logs built around hexagon

What if you took this one step further and made the logs on three sides of the hexagon narrower than the ones on the other three sides?

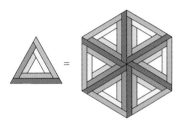

Changing size of logs

Now what would happen if instead of a hexagon, you were to use an equilateral triangle as the center of your Log Cabin block?

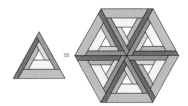

Logs built around triangle

What if you changed the size of the logs on two sides of the triangle?

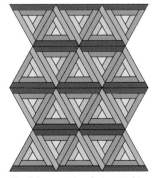

Changing size of logs

What if you laid the triangle blocks out in a different configuration?

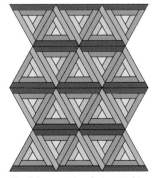

Straight set triangle Log Cabin

What other ideas can you come up with? Read on and we will look at other shapes that can serve as the centers of Log Cabin blocks. Quilt Projects One and Two are made using a hexagon as the center of a Log Cabin block. Both of these projects are small, but they certainly don't have to be. Lesson Four will give you some additional ideas for what to do with small quilts, so you can have fun exploring all the different design ideas and create something to proudly display in your home or to give away to friends or family.

LESSON TWO:
60° Log Cabins

Now that you have started to get an idea of the possibilities of Log Cabin design, let's take it one step further and make the center of the block a 60° diamond. Just as we discussed in Classes 420 and 430, there are many different ways to create a quilt design using 60° diamonds, such as Tumbling Blocks and a wide variety of stars. So what if you took those basic quilt ideas we talked about in those classes and applied them to Log Cabin blocks?

What if you changed the size of the center diamond and made it very small?

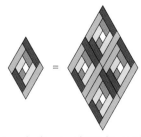

Logs built around 60° diamond

What if you changed the size of the logs on two sides?

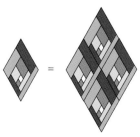

Changing sizes of logs

The design potential is nearly endless, no matter what shape you use as the center of your Log Cabin blocks. Look at the table topper that Carrie designed as the 60° diamond project quilt. The radiating star is created by using a Log Cabin block that is made as a chevron, with logs sewn onto only two sides of the diamond.

LESSON THREE:
45° Log Cabins

Last, but certainly not least, is using 45° diamonds as the center of the Log Cabin blocks. Here are some more ideas to really get your creative juices flowing.

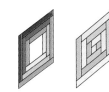

Logs built around 45° diamond

Changing and enlarging diamonds of LeMoyne Star block to Log Cabin blocks

Creating Carpenter's Wheel using Log Cabin blocks

What happens if you change the coloration of the blocks?

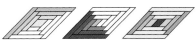

Coloration options on 45° diamonds

What if you change the size of two sides of the logs? What if you alternate Log Cabin blocks with solid diamonds? By making just a few minor changes, you can come up with something totally original. And truly, the shapes are only the beginning. Once the shapes are drawn, the color and width of the logs become the key players in creating some exciting and unique designs!

If you have found making Log Cabins as fun as we have, we are sure that you will want to explore all the different ways this versatile block can be created. Are there other shapes we haven't talked about that could serve as the center of your block? What about a pentagram? Or an octagon? We hope you have enjoyed this exploration into Log Cabins. We will take these ideas even further in Volume 6. Have fun in the meantime!

LESSON FOUR:
Ideas for using small quilts

As you have worked through this series of books, you no doubt have a stack of small quilts that you wonder what you will ever do with. We hope you have used fabric and colors that you really like, and that you are quite attached to the quilts—especially if you have quilted them yourself! Here are some ideas for displaying small quilts.

❋ Don't overlook using small quilts to grace the top of your bed. A quilt doesn't have to be the full size of the bed to be warm and appealing. When turned on the diagonal of a bed, a small quilt can have a lot of impact when laid over pretty sheets, a counterpane, a solid bedspread, or woven blankets.

❋ Carrie's runner *Inlaid Tiles* in Volume 1 (page 84) was made to go over the top of a trunk at the end of her bed. Long, narrow quilts can be used as table runners, bed runners (laid across the end of the bed), or pillow toppers. Bed runners are all the rage in hotels now. A big, beautiful down comforter accented with a colorful long, skinny quilt at the bottom of the bed can be just as effective as a quilt that covers the complete bed—maybe even more so.

❋ Drape a small quilt over the footboard of your bed for display.

❋ Use a small quilt as a nightstand cover, especially if you have a small, three-legged table as a nightstand.

❋ If you are still intimidated about making a full-size quilt, consider making one that fits just the top of the mattress. These are especially good for naps.

❋ If you attempted to make all the blocks in this book, you will no doubt have quite a few stacked up. Consider adding borders or joining coordinating blocks to fit over the pillows on your bed. These are easier to use than pillow shams but will add color and accent to your bedding.

LESSON FIVE:
The quilts
PROJECT ONE: *BIRD'S NESTS*

Bird's Nests

Quilt top size: 28″ × 28″ (side to side)

Yardages needed:

Enough fabric to fussy cut the desired number of center hexagons of the main print

¼ yard dark brown

¼ yard tan

⅓ yard green

⅓ yard blue

Carrie found this fun bird fabric on her travels with Harriet and was excited to find that the birds could be fussy cut to create this fun little table topper for her coffee table.

The centers of these Log Cabin blocks were cut using the large hexagon template from Marti Michell's Perfect Patchwork Templates Set G. If you want to make your own template, draft a hexagon 4″ flat side to flat side.

The logs of this block measure ¾″ when they are finished, making the strips a 1⅜″ cut. This way you will have a little extra, so that when you square up each round of your block, you can trim the strips exactly to width, ensuring you have straight and "square" blocks as you add additional rounds.

For this little quilt, cut the following number of strips:

4 strips of dark brown

5 strips of tan

6 strips of green

7 strips of blue

The method and order of sewing a hexagon-shaped Log Cabin is a little different from that of a square Log Cabin. To save trips back and forth to the ironing board, you can actually place the hexagons along the length of your first log strip and sew them on, leaving ½″ of space between the hexagons.

Sewing hexagons onto first log strip

Cut the hexagons apart. Turn the hexagons and again place on the strip, leaving an unsewn side between where you are about to sew and the log you just sewed on. Once this second log is sewn on, cut the hexagons apart, turn them, again skipping one edge, and sew on a third log of the same color.

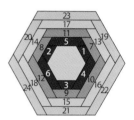

Sewing order for hexagon Log Cabin blocks

Now you can take your blocks to the ironing board and press them, with the seam allowances pressed toward the logs.

To trim your blocks, use a 60° triangle ruler. Lay the ruler down so that the 1¼″ line is lined up with the seamline of one of the logs. Align the right and left edges of the ruler with the edges of the hexagon center and trim away any fabric extending beyond the ruler. Turn the block to align the ruler with the next log and trim; then turn the block a third time and trim.

Trimming hexagon Log Cabin block

Once the first three log ends are trimmed flush with the center, it is back to your sewing machine to add the fourth, fifth, and sixth logs to your block in the same way you added the first three. Sew the hexagons to a strip, cut the hexagons apart off the strip, and turn it to the left to add the next log; repeat again to add the final log.

Once you are done pressing your blocks, it is time to trim the block again. You are trimming it not only to obtain the hexagon shape but also to get the strips to 1¼″ width. Use the 60° triangle ruler to get your hexagon shape and then use your 2½″ × 12½″ ruler with the 60° angle line lined up on one of the seamlines and the 1″ line lined up on the seam of the log you are trimming. Continue in this way all the way around your block. Time to add your second round of logs.

Trimming first-round logs to size

Now that you have the rhythm of sewing on the logs, keep repeating this process until you have as many rounds of logs as you desire around the center hexagon.

When you have trimmed the last round of logs to the 1″ width, it is time to assemble your quilt top. Using the dot system from Marti Michell's templates, mark the dots in each corner of your hexagon blocks. You will be sewing from dot to dot again, just like you did when constructing the *Mosaic Star* table topper in Class 410. Follow that basic method

for finishing the assembly of your quilt top. And that's it. … This is a fast and fun little project you could make as a hostess gift for a friend. Find a whimsical fabric for your center and be creative with your colors! Enjoy!

PROJECT TWO: *PINEAPPLES ALL AROUND*

Pineapples All Around

Quilt top size: 32″ × 32″ (flat side to flat side)

Yardages needed:

⅝ yard large brown floral

⅛ yard (or scraps) small-scale pink floral

¾ yard cream

⅛ yard yellow

⅛ yard brown

⅛ yard pink tonal

⅙ yard green tonal

⅙ yard green floral

Carrie created this little quilt top as a start for a redecorating project she is doing in her guest room. Once quilted, this round quilt will be placed over a table skirt for the night-stand. A bed runner to match will cover the end of the bed. By doing nothing more than purchasing a new solid-color duvet cover, adding a new floor-length table skirt for the night-stand, and making these two items

for the room, these two small touches will make a world of difference in an otherwise neutral-colored room.

The pineapple design that naturally happens when you add the equilateral triangles to three sides of a hexagon is stunning and super easy to create as compared with the real pineapple Log Cabin blocks.

Carrie chose to have the cream tonal fabric as the dominant color of these blocks, so the first row of logs sewn on was a dark color—in this case, yellow. The center hexagon was cut using the small hexagon template from Set G of Marti Michell's Perfect Patchwork Templates. This hexagon is 1¾″ finished size (cut 2¼″ flat side to flat side). To keep the log size balanced with the size of the hexagon, Carrie decided to make the strips half the width of the hexagon, making them ⅞″ finished, 1½″ cut (allow for that magic extra ⅛″ for trimming).

Cut the following strips for this quilt:

1 strip of yellow

2 strips of brown

2 strips of pink

3 strips of green tonal

3 strips of green floral

15 strips of cream

Using the same process as for the *Bird's Nests* Log Cabin, you will be sewing the hexagon to the yellow strip first on three sides of the hexagon. Trim the yellow strips flush with the unsewn edges of the hexagon after you have pressed the logs. The first logs of cream will be added next.

Sewing center hexagon and triangle unit to first cream log

Following the same method as before, sew all six hexagons to the cream strip, leaving a small space between each pair of blocks. Cut the strip to separate the blocks. Rotate the blocks to the next unsewn side, lining them up on the cream strip. Sew.

Once this first round of cream is added, it is time to trim. Once you have cut the straight edges off the strip to reestablish the hexagon shape, align your 2½"-long ruler with both the 60° line on a seamline and the 1⅛" line on the log you are trimming. Repeat this for all six sides. Refer to the photo (page 86) if you need a

refresher. Continue in this manner until you have all five rounds of logs added.

Once all six of the hexagon blocks are finished and trimmed, measure them to make sure they are all the same size and shape. Because of the slight bias you are working with on four sides of the hexagon, these blocks can stretch out of shape slightly when you construct them. If this happens, draft out the finished size of your hexagon on a piece of muslin or freezer paper and block your Log Cabin blocks so they measure correctly.

Use a completed pressed block to make a template for the center large hexagon, as well as for the diamonds that go around the outside edge to make the quilt "round."

For the bed runner that Carrie made for her guest room, she needed 22 of

the hexagon pineapple blocks, 5 solid-piece hexagons, and 12 half-hexagons of the brown floral.

Pineapples All Around bed runner

PROJECT THREE: *PRAYER STAR*

Quilt top size:
63″ (point to point)

Prayer Star

Yardages needed:

- 1⅛ yards white
- ⅙ yard light yellow
- ¼ yard dark yellow
- ¼ yard red print
- ⅓ yard red/black paisley
- ½ yard black

This quilt was made with the colors and thoughts of a Native American prayer wheel. In a prayer wheel, the cardinal directions are each represented by a color, and each color has it own special significance. The logistics of making a quilt that closely approximates a prayer wheel is a little beyond the skill level Carrie felt that she has right now, so this quilt was designed with the colors and ideas of a prayer wheel in mind.

This Log Cabin starts with a 60° diamond in the center that is 1″ larger than the strip size of the logs. It is also sewn as a chevron instead of a "normal" Log Cabin (which has logs on all sides of the center shape).

The basic construction of this Log Cabin is no different from that of the previous hexagon quilts or the three Log Cabin quilts in each of the previous volumes of *Quilter's Academy*. The main difference is that you are only sewing strips on two contiguous sides of the center diamond.

Center diamond and logs of Prayer Star

Once your fabric is straightened, cut a strip from the white fabric for your center diamond 3″ wide. Align a 60° ruler on the strip and cut six 60° diamonds from the strip.

Cut all the strips required of the other colors to speed the process. All the log strips should be cut 2⅛″ wide. Just as in all the other Log Cabin quilts we have made in this series, we are adding an extra ⅛″ to the strip width to allow us to trim the strips to the exact width after they have been sewn to the block.

You will need the following number of strips of each fabric:

- 2 strips of light yellow
- 3 strips of dark yellow (save a strip to cut the six diamonds for the outer star points)
- 3 strips of red print
- 5 strips of red/black paisley (save two strips for the outer star points)
- 7 strips of black (save three strips for the outer star points.)
- 2 strips of white for the outer star points

Sewing order of chevron logs

You are only adding the logs to two sides of the center diamond. It doesn't matter which diamond point you add the logs to, just be sure the logs are on either side of the 60° angle, not the obtuse 120° angle. Once all the diamonds are attached to the log strip, press the seam allowance toward the log strip.

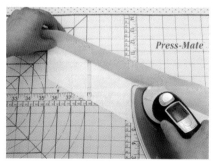

Pressing diamonds attached to first log strip

Don't cut the diamonds apart off the strip as you did with either the hexagons or the square Log Cabins. Because of the sharp angles of the diamonds, it is easier and far more accurate to cut the diamonds off the strip after you have pressed and starched each log strip. Line up your 60° ruler to get an accurate cut. After the diamonds have been separated, you can straighten and trim the edges if necessary.

When you have added all five colors to the chevron diamonds, check the accuracy of the angles of the chevrons. To do this, draft a 60° diamond on a piece of muslin or freezer paper and block your chevrons so they match the drafted template. Because you are dealing with a large amount of bias, taking this bit of extra time to ensure your angles are precise will make the piecing of the final star much easier. Use a little steam and/or starch to press your blocks back into the right angle formation.

Construct the small star points next. These are made by cutting six diamonds from the dark yellow that are the same size as the strip width minus the ⅛″ for trimming—so, they are 2″.

Add the three colors to these diamonds in the same manner you did for the large chevron points.

Once you have the two sets of star points constructed, cut the wide white strips that will complete the star. Cut six 6½″ strips of white and add the shorter side of each large chevron to these strips. For this, three of the strips are needed.

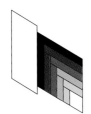

Adding wide strip to chevron

Cut the remaining three strips in half on the center fold and add one of the

small outer star points to each of these half strips.

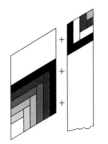

Attaching small star point to white strip

Butting up the seams of the unit you just created (place the seam of the large white strip and the black log of the chevron together), add the star point unit to the chevron.

Attaching small star point unit to chevron

Once the small star point unit is attached to the chevron, trim the corners of the diamonds flush. Sew all of the chevrons together to create the star. Make sure that you align all the seams that meet. Get your graph paper out and have some fun playing with the colors of this great star quilt design.

Think about putting several of these stars together in rows to make a throw or bed-size quilt, or add the wedges to the star to get a great hexagonal table topper. Make your blocks smaller … the possibilities are endless. Have fun creating!

PROJECT FOUR: *WHIRLIGIGS*

Whirligigs

Quilt top size: 53″ × 53″

Yardages needed:

1⅓ yards white

⅛ yard teal

⅙ yard pink

¼ yard red

⅙ yard each of two greens

¼ yard dark teal for border

¾ yard large floral

¼ yard red print

As we were planning the quilts for this book, we got a few new and jazzy lines of fabric into the store, and Carrie got a bug to make one of the quilts out of those lines. *Whirligigs* is the product of that bug. The whimsicalness of the fabric brought to mind those plastic windmills people put in their yards in the summer, and that inspired the color placement of the logs for this version of a Log Cabin block.

This Log Cabin block uses a 45° diamond as the center of the block. The center diamond, which measures 2" finished, is twice as big as the logs. The logs all measure 1" finished and are from strips cut 1⅝".

There is no magic to the order of piecing of this block—the order is just like a square Log Cabin block.

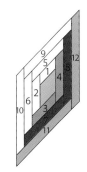

Piecing order of 45° diamond
Log Cabin block

As you did on the chevrons for *Prayer Star,* you will sew all eight diamonds on the log strip and then take the strip and diamonds to the ironing board. Press the seam allowance toward the log strip and cut the diamonds apart (refer to page 89 for a refresher). Again, you must make sure that you have allowed enough fabric at the beginning of each strip for the severe angles of the diamond points, as well as enough room between the

diamonds to get an accurate and clean cut when separating the diamonds on the strip.

Start with two white logs and then two pink logs. Make sure that you refer to the illustration of the order for sewing on the logs. The color placement for this quilt is on the two sides of the obtuse 135° angle at the corners of the diamond, instead of on the acute point as in *Prayer Star.*

Carrie found that using Jan Krentz's Fast2Cut 45° diamond ruler was a lifesaver when measuring to maintain the 45° diamond, as well as when the time came to trim the logs of each round to their proper width.

Using diamond ruler to square up
Log Cabin diamonds

Once you have the knack for aligning the correct ruler lines with your seamlines and trimming your log strips to a 1¼" width, these blocks are extremely easy and fast to sew. Or you can simply use Jan's ruler to create the diamond shape each time you add a log; then use your 2½" ruler with the 45° angle line aligned on a seam and the 1¼" line aligned on the seam of the log you are trimming, as in *Bird's Nests* (page 87).

When you have all eight blocks sewn, create a blocking template on muslin

and double-check the accuracy of your angles. Your diamonds need to match exactly, so use steam and/or starch to coerce the blocks back into shape if needed.

Now it's time to put the diamonds together in the star. We won't go through the order of sewing again, as by now you should be an old pro at putting together LeMoyne Star blocks, no matter what size they are.

Carrie wanted her whirligig to appear to float in a sea of white, so she cut the triangles and corner squares a little larger than necessary to create this effect. The triangles were created from an 18½" square cut in half diagonally in both directions. The corner squares were cut 13" square. This oversizing gives the star about ¾" beyond the points of the diamonds.

The small picture frame border on this quilt is 1" wide finished, and the outer border is 6" finished.

Have fun with this quilt and all the others in this class. We do hope that the ideas we have presented here inspire you to be creative and design your own Log Cabin quilts.

We will revisit Log Cabins in Volume 6, when we will combine block shapes and color variations to create some truly exciting quilts.

Class 470

There are blocks that we don't want to overlook that use 60° or 45° angles but that don't really fit into the classes dedicated exclusively to those angles. So, we are using this class to address them. One of the fun parts of this class is learning how to use partial seams. Piecing can be much like a jigsaw puzzle when it comes to how to put blocks together, and often the standard way is just too complicated to be much fun. If partial seams can be used in the piecing process, then set-in pieces can be sewn in as straight seams. We'll work through several examples to show you how. Then it's on to Peaky and Spike. This pattern unit shows up in so many blocks but can be tricky to get right. We will walk you through the process. You will find that this unit and its close relatives will become a real player when you work through the design ideas in Class 480. This will be a fun class!

LESSON ONE:
Piecing blocks with partial seams

There are a few blocks that present a different challenge when piecing—those with partial seams. They generally have a hexagon or octagon

in the center and the units fit onto the sides, spinning around the center and attached by partial seams. Partial seams are actually very simple to piece. Begin by sewing the first unit onto the center to about the halfway mark. Proceed by adding one piece at a time around the center as usual, working counterclockwise. Once you get around to the original piece, finish stitching this partially sewn seam. This is a different approach to putting the units together. They are fun blocks and worth your time to try.

Pinwheel

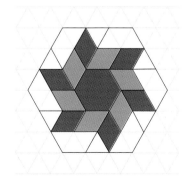

Drafted Pinwheel

This pattern from the 1930s is a variation on six-pointed stars and so much fun to make—and fast! This wonderful block will help you use up scraps or fat quarters. The star points are lying down around the center hexagon instead of pointing outward. This is possible because of the partial seam system of adding sub-units, eliminating set-in seams.

The points of the star are made from strip sets. Position the color for the star points that are against the center hexagon on one side of the strip set and the background fabric on the opposite side. The strip for the points that match the center hexagon is in the center of the strip set. We used a 2″ × 18″ cut strip of each fabric to construct each block. These would be lengthwise-grain strips from a fat quarter.

Join two strips together, press the seam allowances away from the background fabric, measure, and trim if necessary. Add a third strip, adding it to the darkest side. Press in the same direction and trim.

Using a 60° triangle ruler, cut the left end of the strip set at 60°. Measure 2″ down the strip set with a 2½″ straight ruler. Align the 60° triangle ruler lines on the seamlines and make sure both rulers are at the proper position to cut the first 60° angle. Cut the first segment. Continue until you have six segments.

Cutting segments

Cut six 2″ × 6″ rectangles from background fabric. Attach a strip segment to a rectangle, adding it to the top edge. Press toward the background strip. Be sure to align your pieces exactly like those in the illustration. Trim the left side of the background strip even with the left diamond. Trim the right side at a 60° angle, ¼″ beyond the point of the center diamond.

Adding background strip and trimming ends

Let your rulers do the work. Using your 60° triangle ruler, align the seam allowance line on the side of your ruler right at the cut corner of the diamond. Align a cross line with the rectangle seam to ensure your cut is straight. Cut alongside the ruler edge. The ¼″ you need is added exactly.

The center hexagon is cut from a 3½″ × 4″ rectangle. Fold the rectangle in half and have the fold nearest you. Trim each side at a 60° angle, aligning from the bottom corner to the top raw edge.

Fold

Cutting hexagon

Begin constructing the star by aligning the strip side of the strip unit to one side of the hexagon. Be sure that the point of the diamond is offset to form the V for the seam allowance. Stitch the two units together with a partial seam, stopping ½″ from the lower corner of the hexagon. You might want to place a pin at this stopping point. Press the seam toward the strip unit.

Attaching first sub-unit

Working to the left (counter-clockwise), position another strip unit onto the edge of the hexagon. Align the cut edges and butt both seams. Pin if necessary. By butting the seams together, you will position the sub-unit correctly. Stitch the seam end to end and press toward the strip unit.

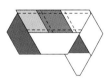

Attaching second strip unit

Continue adding strip units counter-clockwise to the remaining sides of the hexagon. Press carefully after each addition. When you return to the original unit, complete the partial seam.

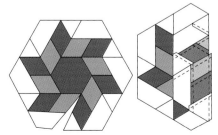

Continue and then finish closing first seam.

Another pretty hexagon pattern is this star. Set-in seams are involved instead of strip piecing, as in Pinwheel. The center starts out with partial seam construction when the trapezoid is added around the hexagon.

Hexagon star

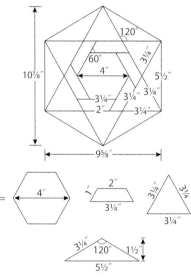

Drafted star and templates needed

The next step is to add the wedge-shaped pieces to the triangles. Once these are paired, repeat the process of sewing on the strips using partial seams. This eliminates sewing the triangles on first, dot to dot, and then setting in the wedge-shaped pieces. How cool is that?

× 6

Attaching triangles to wedges

The process of constructing this star starts the same as for Pinwheel. Starting with one strip, sew to ½″ from the end and then add another strip to the left of the first one, sewing the total seam. Continue until you are back at the beginning, closing the original seam.

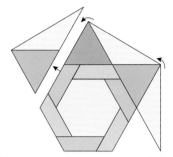

Adding pieces to hexagon counterclockwise

Twisted Star

Twisted Star is constructed in the same manner as Pinwheel, but this time the block comes from an eight-pointed star, causing the points to spin around an octagon.

Drafting the blocks in this lesson is really easy once you know how to draft a basic eight-pointed star. By adding and erasing lines, you will get spinning triangles around an octagon center. Study the illustration to see if you can find the lines that were erased from the basic star. Start by drafting an eight-pointed star any size you want.

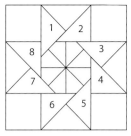

Drafted Twisted Star

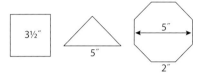

Template sizes for 12″ block

Do you see where the lines for the diamonds have been eliminated in the center and how the points of the triangles form the octagon? Once you visually understand what is happening, start to erase and highlight the lines for the triangles on your drawing.

The construction is straightforward. This is an eight-pointed star with no Y-seams or set-in piecing. Yay!

Once you have selected your color placement, choose which point you want attached to the square and which to the side triangle. Sew these units together, edge to edge, and press as illustrated.

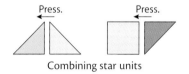

Combining star units

Begin adding a triangle onto one side of the octagon. Sew to within ½″ of the end of the octagon. Press toward the triangle unit.

Attaching first triangle with partial seam

Sew each seam end to end as you add each triangle unit and press toward the added unit after each addition.

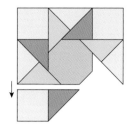

Continue adding star units until you get back to first one.

Once you get back to the beginning, finish the starting seam from where you ended to the end of the triangle. We often find it easier to stitch this seam from the outside edge into the original stitching. The toes of the presser foot are going into a tight area instead of the whole foot sitting on top of the unit.

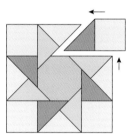

Adding eighth star point

We hope you are delighted with the ease of making these striking blocks. By adding squares in the corners and the side triangles, you get a totally new look from this same block, without much additional sewing.

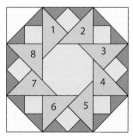

Adding another design element

We have two more to go. Each has more pieces, but they are no more difficult to piece—just a few more steps to take to get them done.

Mosaic

This beauty starts with a 2″ octagon center and adds a second round of triangles around the center. Before we break out the block and piece it, we want to walk you through the drafting. It is difficult to find a pattern for this block, and when there is a pattern, it is seldom the size needed. The fun part of the drafting is that you can make it any size you want, and determining that size is the only math there is!

In keeping with most of the other blocks we have drafted, we will walk you through a 12″ square. There are no magic formulas, but you do need to know how to draft an eight-pointed star. On a 12″ sheet of graph paper (we love the June Tailor 12″ × 12″ Graph-It Paper) draft a 12″ eight-pointed star, without the crossing lines going through the center. We did this in Class 440 (page 50). Draw the dissecting lines lightly, as they will be intersecting triangles where you don't want a heavy line.

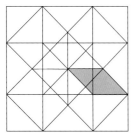
Start with basic eight-pointed star.

The interesting thing about this star is that you draft it working from the outside in. You actually begin by drafting triangles to go around the large octagon in the center of the paper. Looking at the illustration and studying your drawing, do you see the hidden triangles? This will be the template for the large triangles or where you will get your rotary-cutting measurements.

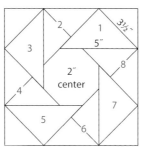
Locating large triangles

The next step is to draw the lines for an eight-pointed star in the center octagon, just as you did for the large square. You are working within the center square area that makes the octagon. Once the lines are drawn, identify the small triangles that encircle the small octagon. Now you have the measurements for these triangles and the center octagon.

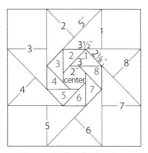
Inner circle of triangles

If the outside square is large enough, you could continue to divide the square down and get more rounds of triangles around an ever-decreasing center octagon. This block is stunning in a 6″ size also.

By changing color placement or not dividing the outside triangle, you get a totally different-looking block, as you can see in B.

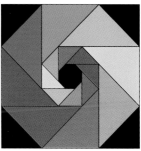
Two different versions of same block—A, B

The large outside triangles can be one piece, or divided and made up of two triangles, one from a color and one from background, for a more refined look. The following measurements are for the block in the photograph. We have included a template for you to use, or you can draft your own. The triangles can be rotary cut from squares, which will ensure that the grainline will remain on the outside edges and prevent the star from getting out of shape.

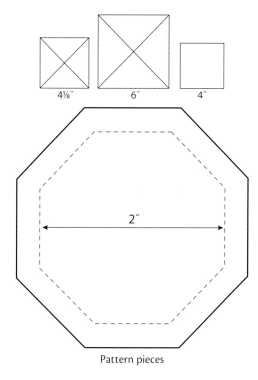

4⅛″   6″   4″

2″

Pattern pieces

Cut an octagon for each star, using the template above. You will need to cut two 4⅛″ squares from two different fabrics and then cut these squares in half diagonally in both directions. In the photo, these are the blue and pink triangles sewn onto the octagon.

You will also need to cut 3 – 6″ squares (the first from background fabric, the other two from two different design fabrics). These are the blue, brown, and cream triangles on the outer part of the block in the photo. Finally, you will need to cut four 4″ squares of background fabric.

Begin by sewing a partial seam (about ½″), joining the long side of a small triangle to one side of the octagon.

Adding first triangle

Working counterclockwise, add another triangle to the octagon, this time sewing the entire length of the seam. With each addition, press toward the triangle. Continue in this manner until all eight triangles are attached. Once the eight triangles are added, complete the original seam.

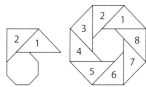

Adding second triangle and progressing around the octagon

Sew the background triangles and corner squares to the design triangles and press away from the background fabric.

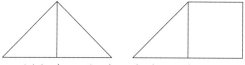

Joining large triangles to background pieces

Repeating the above process, start to add the large triangle units to the octagon unit. Stitch the first seam to ½″ from the end of the small triangle. Move to the left and add a large unit, sewing the complete seam. Continue with the remaining six units. Once the eighth unit is attached, complete the first partial seam.

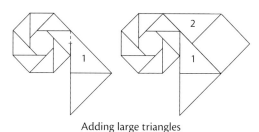

Adding large triangles

Completed block

This block definitely looks harder than it is, but if you are not very accurate, you can get in trouble quickly. Have fun designing with this block and creating a setting for it.

The following blocks are here for you to study and try your hand. Try drafting them in different sizes. Play with color and enjoy making really stunning blocks easily.

The first two blocks, both from the 1930s, are drafted on an 8 × 8 grid, making it somewhat more straightforward to draft than an eight-pointed star. Double Windmill would look wonderful on point with a chain or other detailed connector block. We put four Whirligig blocks together to show the repeat of the corner units when combined side by side. This simple block takes on an entirely different look when multiples are combined.

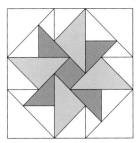

Double Windmill (8 × 8 grid)

1 block

Whirligig (8 × 8 grid)

If you love triangles, this 1936 block named Double Aster is a real beauty. Again, it is drafted on an 8 × 8 grid, building around the center square using partial seams.

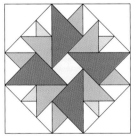

Double Aster

Before we end this lesson, here is some food for thought. You can often avoid set-in piecing by using partial seams. Harriet has long been an admirer of Judy Martin's block designs, but they can appear daunting to piece at first glance. When you study how Judy breaks the sub-units down and joins many units together with partial seams instead of setting in a certain area, the block becomes straightforward. The following blocks were designed by Judy. They can be found in her book *Judy Martin's Ultimate Book of Quilt Block Patterns* (ISBN 0-929589-00-9),

published in 1988. Study these blocks and their components to better understand the concept. And keep this concept in mind when you are designing difficult blocks in the future.

Kitty Corner is based on a 10″ block, and we drafted it on 10-square graph paper. There are five different templates in this block. It looks straightforward enough until you realize that there are four set-in seams. By making sub-units and then using partial seams, you can construct it with all straight seams.

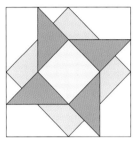

Kitty Corner

Writer's Block isn't a design that spins around a center, but it does have many angles that create places that need set-in piecing. The use of partial seams within the units allows all the pieces to be constructed into two halves. Utilizing partial seams in the last construction step is very like the way we did Feathered Stars in Volume 3, Class 380, Lesson Three (page 106).

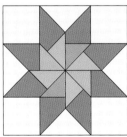

Writer's Block

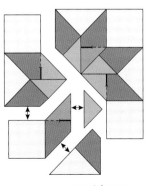

- - - ▬ = partial seam

Block breakout and location of partial seams

LESSON TWO:
Piecing odd shapes

As you get more involved with drafting and working with complex blocks, you are going to run into some pretty odd shapes that might make you think those stars with 45° angles look tame! Take heart; these can be conquered. Once you work through Class 480, you might want to come back here and really work through these techniques, as you will encounter pieces you maybe have never seen before, and you will need to know how to handle them.

As a strip piecer and rotary cutter, Harriet fought with these shapes every time she tried them. She avoided quilts with ice-cream cone and Peaky and Spike shapes in their blocks. These are the blocks that have long, thin right triangles added to two sides of an isosceles triangle (a triangle with two equal-length sides and no right angles). Then along came Perfect Patchwork Templates, with their corner corrections and holes for dot-to-dot placement and sewing guidance. Using these templates made things more accurate, but not all shapes in all sizes are available in these sets. So Harriet was back to drafting—but she made her own templates with extra-heavy template plastic and a ¹⁄₁₆″ hole punch. Now any pattern was under control—until the sewing part. These pesky shapes have their own issues with alignment that are unlike any piece you have worked with up until now. Even with lining up the dots and pinning, it was just as likely not to match as to match. Let's walk through the situation.

It is next to impossible to get any real guidance on how to piece these angles in any of the books on the market, so we experimented and made lots of samples. We think we have worked it out!

Start by drafting the shape of Peaky and Spike and make two sets of templates from heavy plastic. Draw the seamlines onto the plastic and punch a ¹⁄₁₆″ hole at the intersections.

Troublesome shapes: *Left:* Peaky and Spike; *Right:* ice-cream cone

Templates

Hold one set of templates up to the light and match the seamlines and the holes. Tape together to hold them in place. Study each end of the seam. Do you see what is happening?

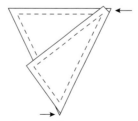

Shapes showing offset seams at both ends

Now use the other set of templates to cut out the fabric to make the unit. Align the fabric so that it looks like the templates you aligned and taped together for guidance. Sew the seam. Start on the right side of the center (spike) piece and sew from the corner

to the lower center. Press toward the side (peaky) piece.

Stitched units

Switch the sides of the templates and tape them together for guidance. Align the remaining peaky onto the remaining side of spike. Peaky will be on top; when you look at the lower seam allowance where both peaky units come together, you will see three different angles. Spike is taller, the first peaky is shorter, and the new peaky is at a different angle yet.

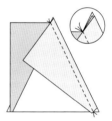

Three angles at beginning of seam

This situation is similar to diamonds and triangles in that the needle needs to start where all of these angles come together. If one of them is off, the point won't be accurate and the ¼″ seam allowance at the raw edge will not be correct.

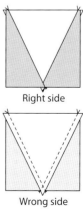

Right side

Wrong side

What units should look like when finished

A unit known as ice-cream cone is another tricky angle to get correct. Again, draft the unit and make a set of templates. This is the best way to get your bearings when positioning the pieces together. Align the seams of the templates as if you are adding the right-side peaky to the cone.

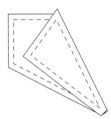
Aligning templates

Align the fabric seams. Start sewing at the intersection of the two units at the wide end. Sew the seam and compare it with the illustration for alignment. Press the seam toward peaky.

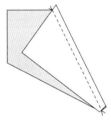
Attaching first side of ice-cream cone unit

Align the second side onto the cone shape. Start sewing at the wide end again, making sure the needle is exactly in the crevice made by the angle of the seams. Press toward the peaky unit again. From the backside of your piece, compare the ends of the seams with the illustrations and measure the distance from the edge to the point. How did you do? If you are having trouble with this, take the time to work it out visually.

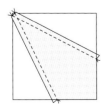
Backside after second side is attached

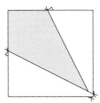
Seam allowances extending from front side

HOW WE REALLY DO IT

Whether you like working with the dot-to-dot system or the sample template system, we have discovered a really slick way to take a bit of the guesswork out of the alignment part of making these units. Once we discovered it, we wondered whether we should even bother with all the other instructions. But since these are teaching manuals, we decided that there is a place for knowledge of all the different approaches.

When we had you place the skinny template onto the isosceles triangle in the first part of the lesson, you could see the offset of the seam allowances. This time, when you overlay the templates and match the seam allowances, tape them together so they don't slip. You will see where the tips of each triangle template extend beyond the edge of the other template. Using either a pair of sharp scissors or your rotary cutter, trim away the points on both templates. If you cut around the templates, the point will be trimmed before you start to sew. If you rotary cut the pieces, lay the template over the cut fabric unit and carefully align all the edges. Carefully trim away the excess fabric at the points. Now when you align the fabric pieces for sewing, the tips are cut at exactly the same angles. You don't need to guess about whether the points are in just the right place. It is so exciting to keep learning new ways to work through problem pieces!

Trimming templates

LESSON THREE:
Matching points another way

This will be the shortest lesson in the book. But it is something that we do all the time and have not really put much emphasis on. Have you found that when you are sewing a long seam with many points that need to match, you can only see half of them from the side of the block that is facing up? There are so many times that we wind up picking out parts of the seam to correct the points that did not come out correctly, simply because we could not see where to exactly put the needle.

What we do many times in this situation is sew a partial seam on one side to match the points that we can see; then we turn the seam over and join the stitching from the other side, again working with the points where we can see them. Whenever there is a crossroads that lets you see the point you need to hit, have that side up when sewing.

LESSON FOUR:

The quilts

PROJECT ONE: *PINWHEEL*

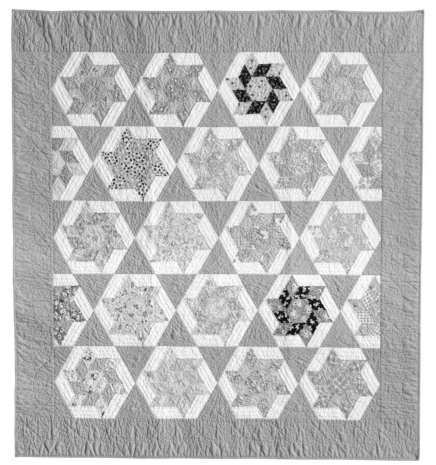

Pinwheel

We chose this quilt for the project in this class because it is an easy block to make but looks more complicated than it really is. We thought that after all you have been through with the extreme detail in the piecing of the previous classes, you needed a respite for a while. If you made the sample block in Lesson One, you already know how to construct the blocks. If you did not make a sample, follow the instructions (page 92) to construct the 22 blocks needed for this small quilt.

Quilt top size: 42″ × 45″ (without borders)

Block size: 9″

Blocks: 22

Yardages needed:

22 assorted light medium prints*

22 assorted medium prints*

1 yard white (this could be a light print or a shirting-type fabric)

2¼ yards green (includes borders on lengthwise grain)

For blocks, cut:

1 – 2″ × 18″ strip from each light medium print

1 – 2″ × 18″ strip from each medium print

1 – 3½″ × 4″ rectangle from each medium print (center hexagon)

22 – 2″ × 18″ strips white

22 – 2″ × 6″ strips white

These blocks are really pretty when made scrappy, and they need very little fabric. If you have a stash of fat quarters, this is a good time to break into it. If not, you can purchase either ⅛-yard pieces, fat eights, or fat quarters of the prints.

Follow the instructions (page 93) to make the strip sets using the cut fabrics. Follow through the instructions until you have 22 blocks finished.

Once the blocks are finished, position them on the design wall to decide on color placement. You will have five rows of blocks. Rows 1, 3, and 5 have four blocks in each row. Rows 2 and 4 have five blocks each. The blocks at each end of these rows will be cut in half before borders are added.

> *note* If you don't like the idea of cutting a block in half, you can add wedges of the background fabric, as we did for several of the earlier quilts. Refer back to both quilts in Class 430, Lesson Four (page 40) for instructions for measuring and inserting these wedges.

Using the green fabric, cut 46 equilateral triangles that measure 5¼″ on each side. Draft, add seam allowances, and make a template, or mark a 60° ruler to this size. Square off the points so that they match up perfectly to the angle of the blocks. (Use #44 of Set G of Perfect Patchwork Templates if you have them.) Cut the fabric into strips 5″ wide. You will get nine triangles from each strip, so you will need to cut five strips. Mark the dots at the corners for sewing alignment. Place the triangles on the design wall between the blocks and at the ends of Rows 1, 3, and 5. Use the illustration as a guide for placement.

Pinwheel layout

We will construct this quilt by rows. If you want to explore your options for sewing the rows together, refer to Class 430, Lesson Four, Project Two: Diamond Starburst (page 48). We will to walk you through making straight rows across the width of the quilt. Following the above diagram, begin adding triangles to the Pinwheel blocks. Attach the first triangle starting at the lower left edge of the first block. Add another triangle to this block directly across from the first one—the top right side. Continue adding triangles to the remaining blocks in this row in the same manner. Add the top left corner to the first block in the row, and then the bottom right corner of the fourth block. Sew the units together, carefully aligning the points at the intersection. You do not have to sew dot to dot with this quilt. Instead, sew raw edge to raw edge of each triangle through the blocks.

Continue following the diagram until all the rows are constructed. Carefully match the intersecting triangles to get perfect points where they cross at the intersection. Once the rows are constructed, it is time to join the rows. Align the row, pinning at the intersections of the triangles. Remember how the 60° seams aligned when you made the Diamond Starburst quilt in Class 430? Repeat that alignment for Pinwheel. The seam on top should align with the raw edge of the lower seam. If you have kept your seam allowance accurate, they will align easily. Pin through both layers, running the pin into both layers

exactly where the seams intersect. Once the row is pinned, stitch. Open the seam and check your intersections. If they are slightly spread apart, take a slightly deeper seam and check again.

Continue until all five rows are joined. Press the quilt top well and starch lightly to keep the seams flat and sharp.

You will now cut the blocks that extend beyond the edge in half, as well as the triangles at the ends of the odd-numbered rows. Using a large square ruler, position it in one corner and align it with the top edge of the blocks in Row 1 and ¼″ from the intersecting seams of the triangles along the side. Trim. Repeat for all four sides of the quilt top.

Measure for the borders to determine the length to cut. If you prefer to cut your borders on the lengthwise grain, you will need more yardage. We figured the yardage for lengthwise strips taken from the yardage before cutting the triangles. If you prefer to cut the borders crosswise, refer to Volume 1, Class 180, Lesson Three (page 95) for a review of splicing borders on the diagonal.

Attach the side borders first and press. Measure for the top and bottom borders through the center of the quilt and cut borders. Attach to the top and bottom of the quilt top.

This is a perfect style of quilt to add a simple appliqué vine and flowers to the corners if you want to dress it up a bit. Small hexagon flowers would also be cute in the border.

PROJECT TWO: *AMISH PASTURES*

Amish Pastures

This quilt utilizes the Storm at Sea pattern. It is small and very versatile and gives you a chance to try your hand at the Peaky and Spike units. We chose to fussy cut a wonderful fabric printed with Amish farm scenes for the square-in-a-square blocks, and we used rich greens to surround these pictures to make the pastures. Traditionally the position of the green is blue and represents the water of the sea, and the curves created by the angles represent the storm. We went for gently waving grass in a summer breeze. This would be a great pattern for any of the fun panel fabrics that are available: fishing, horses, Christmas, baby motifs, kitchen themes, and so on.

Quilt top size: 30″ × 30″ (without borders)

Blocks: There really isn't a true block for this quilt, as the pattern develops by sharing sides within the setting. If you measure one full block, it is 12″ in our quilt. You will be constructing units instead of blocks.

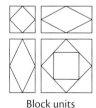

Block units

Yardages needed:

We suggest that you find the fabric you want to use and determine how big the center square will have to be cut. This will determine the size of all the

other units. It is not possible to list yardages for that part of the quilt as it varies by size.

Also, once you have the center square size determined, we trust that you will be able to figure the remaining yardage needed for the rest of the quilt. After all, this is at the end of your senior year, and we have addressed yardage throughout the previous three books. We have faith in you!

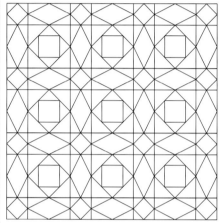

Line drawing of Storm at Sea layout

Placement of units in quilt top

This pattern is interesting to draft, as you can make it work with almost any size panel print or center square you need or want. Let's look at how we drafted our size: We chose a pretty, allover farm scene fabric, but the sizes of the topics we wanted to fussy cut were erratic. Taking an average size, we cut a plastic template, including seam allowance, and placed it over the subjects. With the size established, we could draft the pattern. Our center square for the square-in-a-square block finishes at 4¼″. When this square is placed on point, we need the diagonal measurement. This should be easy by this time:

$$4.25'' \times 1.414 = 6''$$

The center of the block is 6″. Referring back to Volume 3, Class 330, Lesson Three (page 38), we know that we need to cut the center square 4¾″ (includes seam allowances) and the corner triangles from two squares cut 4⅜″, each cut in half diagonally.

Center and sew a triangle onto two opposite sides of the large square. Press and cut the points off, making them even with the square. Repeat for the opposite side. Using a Precision Trimmer, trim to 6½″, checking that the points are ¼″ from the cut edge.

If the above squares are 6″, the side rectangle units would be 6″ by half as wide, or 3″. Draw a rectangle 6″ × 3″ on a sheet of graph paper. Find the center points on each side of the rectangle. Connect these points to develop the lines for the inner diamond and the corner pieces.

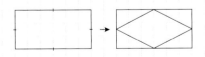

Drafting side units

tip Can you see how you can make this block any size you need? This is especially handy when working with panels or allover prints that you want to fussy cut. Determine the size of the center square needed. The side units are that measurement in one direction and one-half that measurement in the other. The corner units are the smaller measurement, square. And who said drafting was hard?

Carefully cut out the diamond unit and one corner unit exactly on the drawn line. Glue these patterns onto a piece of extra-heavy template plastic. Add seam allowances to the templates and cut them out. Following the instructions above, place the templates together and trim the corners for easy placement and seam alignment.

The corners are another smaller square in a square. The finished square is 3″. The diagonal measurement of the inside square is 3″; so the squares are cut 2⅛″ plus seam allowance:

$$3'' \div 1.414 = 2.12'' = 2\tfrac{1}{8}''$$

Again, make a template 2⅝″ square to use for fussy cutting the small inner squares. The chart in Volume 3 (page 38) tells you that the corner triangles come from two squares cut 2⅞″ that are then cut in half diagonally. Construct these square-in-a-square units the same as the larger center one.

For this size quilt top, make:

9 large center square-in-a-square units

16 small corner square-in-a-square units

24 diamond units

Once the units are constructed, lay out the pieces on the design wall and make sure everything is upright. You can approach the joining process a couple of different ways by looking at how the blocks blend together.

Options:

✳ Sew rows together, starting at the top and working down.

✳ Make the four corner blocks and then construct the units needed to join them.

✳ Working vertically, construct wide units that equal the corner blocks for both the right and left side of the quilt top. Construct the narrow band that joins them together last and join both larger units to either side.

Obviously, it is your decision how to plan the piecing. There are six points coming together within every seam, so take your time and position them carefully for accuracy. Pinning is necessary for this project. Insert a pin directly into the point on the top unit and run it through to the bottom layer, inserting it exactly into the point. Hold tight and insert another pin, taking a stitch this time and having the point come out exactly in both points. Remove the first pin.

Be sure that you alternate the seams as you press them from row to row. Once the top is finished, add any borders that are appropriate for your fabric choices.

Class 480 will take you into the amazing world of changing grids and proportions, where you will find these types of units appear everywhere. We hope you take the time to master these odd shapes so that the drawings in the next class do not look so intimidating.

Class 480

You made it to the best part! All the work you have done and skills you have achieved up to this point are all going to come into play in this class.

This class is a follow-up to Volume 3, Class 330, Lesson Five (page 41). If you worked through that lesson, we are sure you had some fun seeing blocks repeated and colored in new inventive ways. In this class, we expand on the ideas presented in Volume 3. You will now learn to make your own original blocks, using graph paper and the different component parts of blocks. This is a lost art in this age of computer-aided drafting. If you just can't get away from your computer, you can adapt these ideas to your favorite CAD program. Many of us have allowed our creative brains to go to sleep and allow an electronic box to have all the fun. Our goal here is to turn you on to getting into the right side of your brain and learning to play. Very few of us can look at a blank sheet of paper or a stack of fabric, start from nothing, and make something wonderful. We need a road map. Here are fun, easy ways to be creative with graph paper. And now that you know drafting much better and can work with templates, the fun you can have with this class is endless.

LESSON ONE:
Understanding grids

So many of us think we are not artistic, but we are all born with the ability to be creative. It is usually just a matter of exploring creativity a couple of times to see that our mind is full of wonderful original ideas. All the women mentioned throughout this book have given us confidence through their work. Everything you need to know to design pieced quilts can be drawn on graph paper! You don't have to be good at math or have drafting skills. The quilts you come up with can be as simple or as intricate and challenging as you want. And now that you have pieced difficult blocks as well as learned to draft them to any size and make templates to work with, anything you come up with in this class will be doable!

The system we will walk you through uses unit blocks—basic repeating patterns. Let's get started.

We have been teaching you about units—or grids—throughout all four volumes of this course. The first step to designing your own blocks is to find a grid you like, a block you would like to start with, or a grid that is divisible into ruler-happy numbers for the block size you want or need.

The 2 × 2 base grid is the basis for other grids that are formed by dividing the squares of the base grid repeatedly in half. This is probably the largest category of base grids in quiltmaking. Quilters often refer to 2 × 2 blocks as "four-patch" because of the four squares that make up the grid. Within this category are the 4 × 4 grid, 8 × 8 grid, 16 × 16 grid, 32 × 32 grid, and 64 × 64 grid. The higher numbers tend to indicate a large area of design. You can get deeply involved in these patterns when you start to repeat and mirror your units.

2 × 2

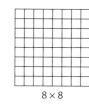
4 × 4

8 × 8

16 × 16

Grids based on 2 × 2

The 3 × 3 base grid category includes all blocks based on a grid of three squares across and three squares down. Included in this category is the quilter's term "nine-patch," but we will refer to them as 3 × 3 design grid. Within this category are 6 × 6, 12 × 12, 24 × 24, and 48 × 48 grid blocks.

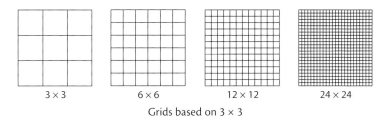

Grids based on 3 × 3

The 5 × 5 base grids include 10 × 10, 20 × 20, and 40 × 40.

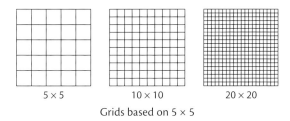

Grids based on 5 × 5

The 7 × 7 base grids include 14 × 14, 28 × 28, and 56 × 56.

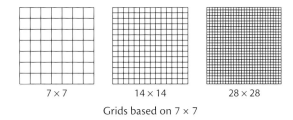

Grids based on 7 × 7

The 9 × 9 base grid is a multiple of three. Many of the designs from this category are similar to those in the 3 × 3 category. We have included 9 × 9 as a category because of the number of blocks that are subdivided beyond 3 × 3. The 9 × 9 grid makes it easier to draw in the subdivisions. The 18 × 18 and 36 × 36 grids are in this group. Log Cabin blocks tend to fall into this category.

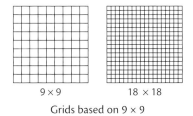

Grids based on 9 × 9

The grids continue with 11 × 11, 13 × 13, and 15 × 15 base grids.

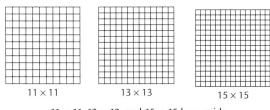

11 × 11, 13 × 13, and 15 × 15 base grids

We hope you have a better understanding of the system of grids and will put them to work for you. To begin, let's keep it simple and work with empty 3 × 3 base grid blocks. Start by drawing several empty blocks on graph paper. If you have our graph paper packet, you will find 3, 6, and 9 squares to the inch. When you subdivide the units within each square, you will appreciate having more lines within the square to work with. If you have a photocopy machine, it will be your best friend through this process and will save you tons of time.

LESSON TWO:
Design and drafting

DESIGNING ON GRAPH PAPER

In 1983, Judy Martin wrote a book that holds many of the answers to becoming comfortable with designing quilt patterns—*Patchworkbook: Easy Lessons for Creative Quilt Design and Construction* (ISBN 0-684-17945-8). It is a formula for steps to take to create original and unique quilt designs. This book has been out of print for years, but we feel it is well worth the hunt and expense of finding a used copy and to work through it if this process really fascinates you.

Patchworkbook presented a formula for how to experience the joy of creating your own original designs without being a graphic artist or having any art background. By the late 1980s and early 1990s, Mary Ellen Hopkins and Marti Michell were exploring similar ideas and teaching them at the It's Okay If You Sit On My Quilt seminars. Harriet went to more than fifteen of these seminars and was well trained to think outside the box. Many of the ideas in this class are from those seminars. The early 1990s were a heyday for originality. But then came the computers. Now we don't want to play with paper and colored pencils anymore. What a loss for our creative brains.

Well, we want to wake those creative juices up again and show you how much fun this can be. We will start with an empty 3 × 3 grid block.

Empty nine-patch block

A 3 × 3 grid is made up of squares arranged so that there are corners, middles, and a center. Every time something is added to one of these units, a new block is created, and a new name is assigned. Look at the progression of the empty 3 × 3 grid blocks when simple lines are added.

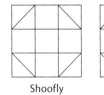

Shoofly · Churn Dash · North Wind · Checkerboard

Stepping Stones · Weathervane · 54-40 or Fight · Mona's Choice · Faceted Star

Are you starting to see the progression of the changes? We start with a very simple block with nine empty squares. By adding a diagonal line through each of the corners, we get Shoofly. Churn Dash is similar to Shoofly, but the center is light and the middle squares have been divided in half. When we cross all but two squares with a diagonal line, we create North Wind. If four-patch units are placed in the corners, we have Checkerboard, but if we use triangles in the middle blocks and another four-patch in the center, we get Stepping Stones. These are all very standard old blocks that have been used by generations of quilters.

The addition of shapes other than triangles and squares can really give a 3 × 3 grid block impact. Weathervane has house units in the middles, and the corners have taken the four-patch and added triangles to two of the four-patches. 54-40 or Fight changes the units in the middle from house units to Peaky and Spike—a name coined by Doreen Speckmann that has stuck. Mona's Choice and Faceted Star have even more unusual shapes in all the spaces. Who would have thought that drawing lines in empty boxes could produce such different results? The thing is, this is just the tip of the iceberg. It is limitless where you can go with this concept. This is just thinking of 3 × 3 grid units. There are also all the other base grids to work with, as shown earlier.

Let's start by looking at the components that make up the blocks illustrated at left. You can see that the shapes in the various squares can be rotated, mirrored, and spun around the center to totally change the look of the block.

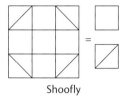

Shoofly

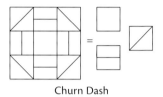

Churn Dash

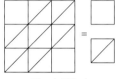

North Wind

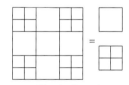

Checkerboard

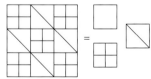

Stepping Stones

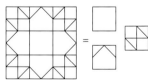

Weathervane

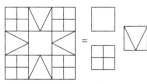

54-40 or Fight

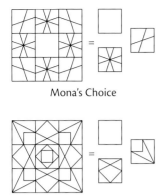

Mona's Choice

Faceted Star

Okay, you have seen what simple shapes can do to the grid, but what if you had a whole toolbox of shapes to try in these positions? After you have learned to break a block down into grids and shapes, you can start to make it your own. You can customize a standard block to be uniquely yours with a little time playing with color, pattern, proportion, and orientation. Using the following basic components, start to fill in the empty spaces of *your* blocks.

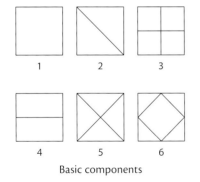

Basic components

Add some complexity to the blocks and play with some or all of these components as you draw out different patterns. You might want to draw your empty blocks larger when adding the more complex units. It will be easier to distinguish the shapes and to color the blocks later in the exercise.

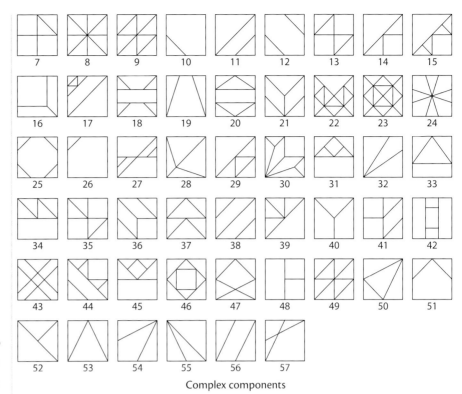

Complex components

> **tip** Harriet found many of these unusual components by going through *The Quilter's Album of Blocks & Borders* by Jinny Beyer (ISBN 978-0914440925). It is the most complete block book on the market and is beautifully done. We think every quilter needs this book on the shelf—especially if you are interested in pursuing this type of drafting and design work. It is extremely inspirational.

Many of the blocks you have created probably have a name already and can be found in books that list blocks by name and grid. Don't get discouraged, as this is only the beginning. Here are six patterns that we came up with. We have listed the component numbers underneath the block for reference.

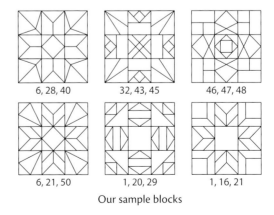

Our sample blocks

Mix and match, repeat, mirror, spin, or anything else you can think of. If you played with the design concepts in Volume 3, where we had you make up two-bell blocks and photocopy them to create repeats, use that same idea here. If you have at least four of each of the components photocopied and cut into small squares, you can position them on 3 × 3 graph paper and save a lot of time and paper drawing and erasing.

You do not have to work with only the components. You can simply add or erase lines from a pattern you already like to make the changes. Or, if you have created a block you like but you don't like a particular line or several lines, you can always erase them. You can draw in more lines than the components give to get another look. What you are creating are patterns—the arrangement of the shapes in the block.

Let's keep going with the pattern ideas. What if you added a round of squares around the block itself—somewhat like a border—and added more units within that area.

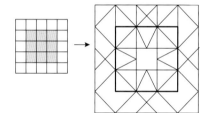

Changing basic block

Let's try a five-patch pattern. As you look at the five-patch, imagine there is a crossbar that goes through because of the uneven squares. What if you worked with the crossbar as a separate unit and then surrounded it with other components?

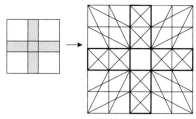

Working with five-patch block

Another form of working with components is the block itself. Many blocks, especially two-bell blocks (Volume 3, Class 330, Lesson Five), have endless potential. As a review, and for the next step, let's work with a simple block—Birds in the Air—and build it into various components. North Wind is another great block to make into components. Once you have come up with every combination you can conceive of, number them. Make a bunch of photocopies of them, cut the units out, and start to arrange them in whatever order you choose. Squint at the pattern as it emerges and you will start to see some very interesting secondary shapes and designs emerge. Look for chains, medallions, stars, arrowheads, and so on, as you make the combinations. If nothing is appearing, replace some of the component units or start over.

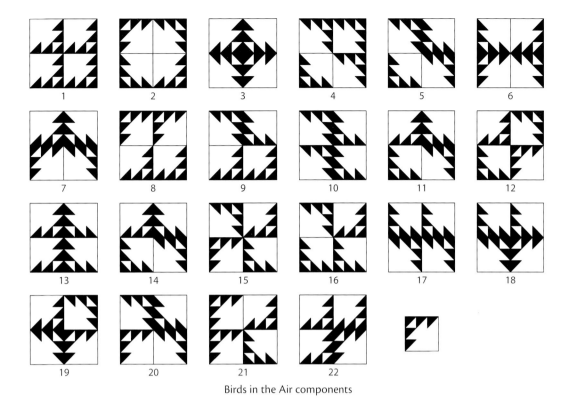

Birds in the Air components

There are four different combinations of these components using mirror imaging, spinning, and random placement of the units. As you squint at them, do you see patterns emerge from all the different angles? We will continue to work with this idea further on in the lesson.

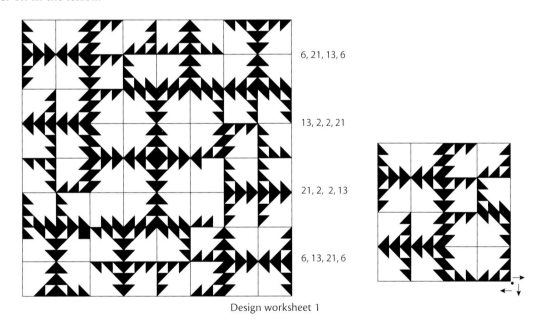

6, 21, 13, 6

13, 2, 2, 21

21, 2, 2, 13

6, 13, 21, 6

Design worksheet 1

Does this pattern look totally random to you? It is actually the same four components in the same configuration spinning clockwise around the center point. Do you see the spinning lines? What would color do to accentuate some of the stronger design elements? Or do you just not like it and want to move on?

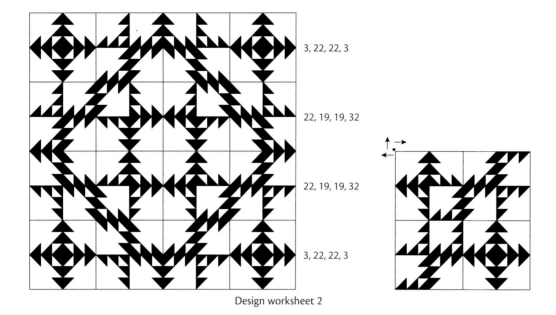

3, 22, 22, 3

22, 19, 19, 32

22, 19, 19, 32

3, 22, 22, 3

Design worksheet 2

This time there are fewer components used, and the setting is very symmetrical. The quadrant is mirrored in both directions instead of spinning as in design worksheet 1. Do you see the medallion in the center? We thought this pattern has the look of a Native American Indian blanket. We are excited to play with colors.

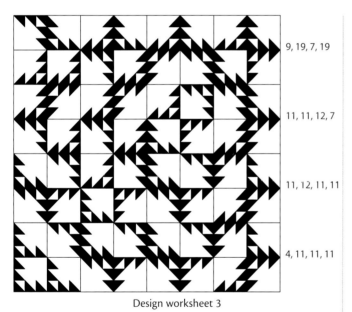

9, 19, 7, 19

11, 11, 12, 7

11, 12, 11, 11

4, 11, 11, 11

Design worksheet 3

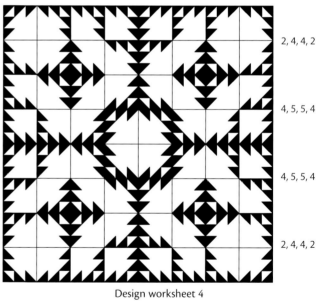

2, 4, 4, 2

4, 5, 5, 4

4, 5, 5, 4

2, 4, 4, 2

Design worksheet 4

This pattern doesn't have symmetry, but there is a hint of interlocking squares when you squint. It might be fun to clean up some areas (erase some elements) and have a more striped look.

This is another really nice symmetrical design with some wonderful focal points in the corners and the center. This is worthy of the time it will take to color.

Now that you have played with components and their arrangement, the fun gets even better. If you just don't have time to have a cup of tea and play with colored pencils, you could easily adapt these concepts to your computer if that suits you better.

LESSON THREE:
Block coloring

The next step is to choose colors for your blocks or combination of blocks. Put your taste and style into the design. But don't stop with color. Once you choose the colors for various positions in the design, you can choose the fabric—looking at print scale and type as well as textures and stripes—to add even more variety or continuity. Refer to Volume 1, Class 160, Lesson One (pages 67–71), for a review of fabric types.

Study the illustrations at top right. We have colored the same block two different ways. But during the coloring process, we found that by changing one line in each corner in one block led to a very different outcome. We wouldn't have known this before we started to color in the spaces.

There are several ways to approach coloring in the block:

❋ If you have combined several blocks or many components together, treat the design as one total unit. If there are three components or blocks across and three down, color it as if it were one big nine-patch.

❋ When you squint at your design or pattern, do you see that some elements stand out more than others? Are there too many confusing pieces around these elements to focus on the important part? Try erasing some of the lines to clean up the area. This will make a more plain background and put the focus where you want it.

❋ Don't forget the saying, if in doubt, put it on point. We hope you really put this into practice in Volume 2, where we dealt exclusively with diagonal sets. Once the pattern is on point, eliminate the corners and concentrate on the diagonal center.

Can you come up with more ideas? Put these processes to work on a few of the patterns you created in the last lesson. You will be amazed at how much color placement will change the look of your blocks. Once the colors are in an arrangement you really like, work through a few actual mock-ups with fabric or photocopied fabric (see Volume 1, Class 150, Lesson Four, page 54). This will help you see if the print or scale actually translates to what you want.

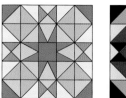
Same block colored two different ways

Below are color versions of most of the patterns we drafted so that you can see how much color plays a part of design. Lines alone drawn in squares give no depth, but with the addition of color, you start to see movement and repeats emerge. The first blocks we worked with are a bit simple and plain. As we added more lines and broke the space more erratically, the blocks became much more interesting.

Blocks with color

Once you have your blocks colored in, get out your mirrors and look at what happens when they are repeated. Don't just put the mirrors in the corner and get a block-to-block repeat—move the mirrors around. We found that when we divided the block in an unusual place, the design took on the look of a kaleidoscope. New patterns emerged that were much more exciting than the original. In this case, you could copy the block, cut it apart in the new formation, and create something totally original.

Let's return to a couple of the illustrations we did with the Birds in the Air components. As we were playing with colors, some really wonderful patterns emerged. It is a 24-unit (-patch) design of the 3 × 3 unit family.

Design worksheet 4, colored

We did the first coloring on top of a very light photocopy of our drawing. You will be able to see in your drawings where lines should be added or eliminated. Once you have the coloring done, photocopy the pattern and cut it apart to get the new components that you will piece. The color placement becomes a part of each component.

New components

Once the pattern is colored and then broken out, you can identify all the elements that need to be pieced to put it together. Determine a grid size depending on the size of the quilt you want, and you will be ready to figure yardage. If you want a 2″ grid, the quilt would finish at 48″ square. If the grid is 2½″, it would be 60″. And if you bumped it up to a 3″ grid, you would get a 72″ quilt.

The second design is also taken from one of the seminar drawings. It is also a 24-unit (-patch) design of the 3 × 3 unit family.

Design worksheet 2, colored

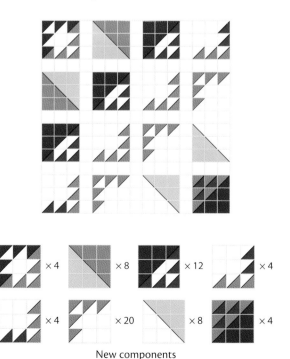

New components

The sizing is the same for Design worksheets 4 and 2. Now that you see how basic the piecing is, but how striking the quilt is, we do hope that you are inspired to put some time and effort into designing your own quilt tops.

The above designs are mainly half-square triangle units. We will move onto more difficult piecing in the next process.

Now that you have learned to make and work with templates, as well as set in pieced blocks, your design potential is very high. Don't let all your newfound knowledge go to waste.

LESSON FOUR:
Proportions

Now the fun really starts. Traditional blocks are generally drawn on an even square grid, but what if we change parts of the block by enlarging or reducing different grids—compressing some grids and stretching others? Instead of squares, let's shift the grid by drawing a rectangular or diamond-shaped grid. Let's explore how this works. The easiest way to play with this concept is to use a variety of different grid papers. We suggest that you get a package of the graph paper made for this series of books, which has grids from 3 × 3 to 10 × 10 squares per inch (see Resources, page 128).

You can change the proportions of the block by redrawing the designs using different-sized squares or rectangles instead of a grid of same-sized squares. The block does not have to stay symmetrical. The top can be small and the bottom large. One corner can be narrow and the rest of the block larger. The center can be skinny or wide, and the same can happen with the corners. Here are a few examples. Can you come up with more?

These three blocks are an example of different grid changes. The first block—Sawtooth Patchwork from 1897—is a 3 × 3 grid block. The proportion is changed by changing the spacing on graph paper. Instead of three equal divisions, the corners are twice as wide as the center. The center units are now tall and narrow in proportion to the square corners.

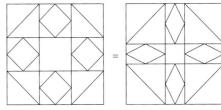
Sawtooth Patchwork

Hovering Hawks is typically a 2 × 2 grid, or what we call a four-patch. We redrafted the grid for an orientation of 2 squares, 2 squares, 1 square, and 1 square. The right lower side of the block is compressed and the top left side is stretched. As you get further into this idea, you will see this block drafted in several different grid proportions.

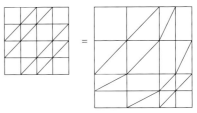
Hovering Hawks

Variable Star is also a typical four-patch design, but there are so many ways to redraft it. Here we have turned it into a rectangle by dividing the grid along the top into 2 squares, 3 squares, 1 square, and 2 squares. Along the length, all four grids have been divided into 3 squares each. This gives a very distorted look to the star. But when they are mirrored and repeated, all kinds of fun things start to happen.

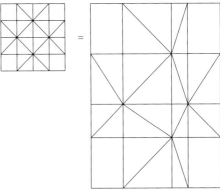
Variable Star

Next, take this new block and combine it with more of itself. The following illustrations show five drawings of Variable Star blocks. A–E show the changes to the block grid. We photocopied these blocks and placed four of them together to make a larger block. When they are side by side, the lines start to create even more new internal lines, and the design takes on a totally unexpected turn.

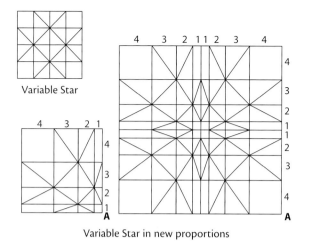

Variable Star

Variable Star in new proportions

How about adding rectangles as well as squares?

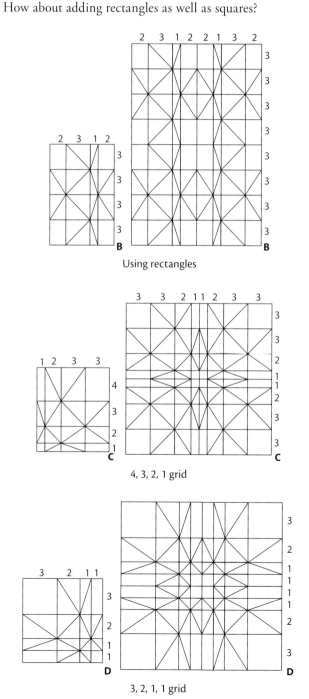

Using rectangles

4, 3, 2, 1 grid

3, 2, 1, 1 grid

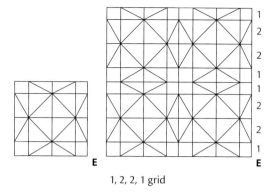

1, 2, 2, 1 grid

The preceding designs are four blocks joined together. What happens if you place four of these larger blocks together? Now the quilt design really starts to emerge. You start to see secondary patterns. As you start to color these in, you will likely erase some lines to open up areas and add lines to other areas to create new shapes.

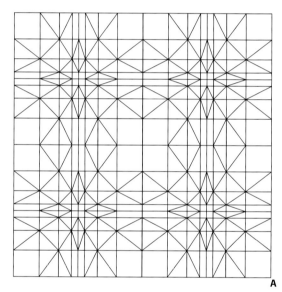

Variable Star × 16—A expanded

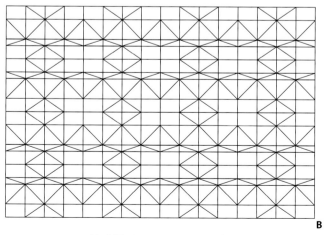

Variable Star × 16—B expanded

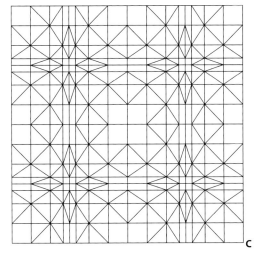

Variable Star × 16—C expanded

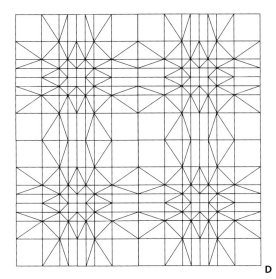

Variable Star × 16—D expanded

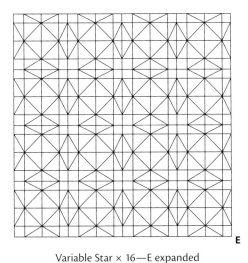

Variable Star × 16—E expanded

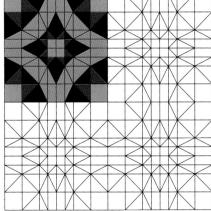

One block of four, colored

Another version colored as one large block

We want you to examine the following graphic carefully. It is the Storm at Sea block, but it incorporates three different sizes of Storm at Sea blocks, as well as a different layout for the block. If you look at the block, you see it is surrounded with the diamond unit on all sides and then set side by side in the interior of the design. The border is the traditional layout of the block but in a smaller grid. Finally, the units are colored and shaded to create a medallion feel. This quilt was designed by Linda Franz. Linda has written an entire design book on the Storm at Sea block, and she shows how to utilize all the different ideas given in this class using this wonderful block. Check out her work at her website, www.inklingo.com.

Storm at Sea by Linda Franz

We have gone through the same steps with Hovering Hawks. This design proved very versatile.

Hovering Hawks block

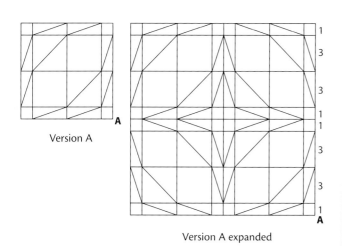

Version A

Version A expanded

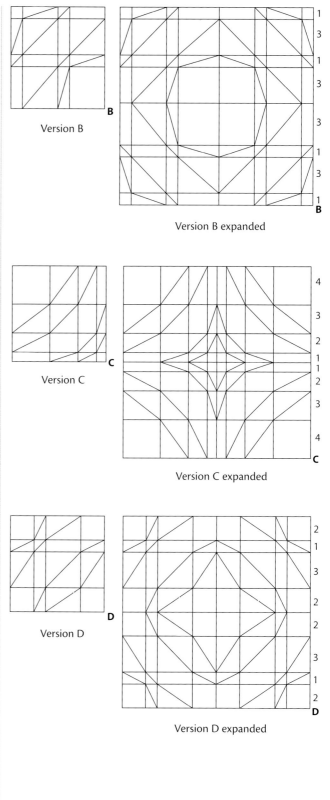

Version B

Version B expanded

Version C

Version C expanded

Version D

Version D expanded

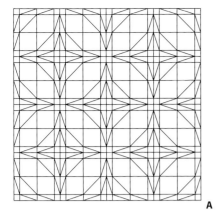

Version A × four blocks

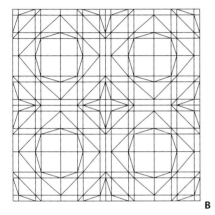

Version B × four blocks

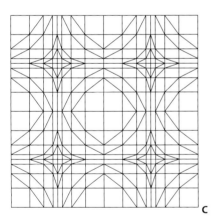

Version C × four blocks

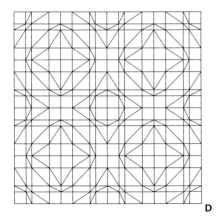

Version D × four blocks

By adding one more grid and one more line to Hovering Hawks, we got a block named Ocean Waves, which gave us more defined circles.

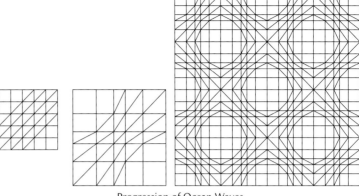

Progression of Ocean Waves

LESSON FIVE:
Block orientation

This is where we refer you back to Volume 2, Class 250 (page 54) for ideas about settings. Also, play with the ideas in Volume 2, Class 260 (page 82) for ideas about putting blocks on point. Any of these designs could be put on point or have lines in the corners erased to get a whole new look.

Another tool to consider putting into play when designing your own patterns is symmetry. Symmetry is defined as

❋ The property of being the same or corresponding on both sides of a central dividing line

❋ Harmony or beauty of form that results from balanced proportions

❋ A correspondence in the position of pairs of points of a geometric object that are equally positioned about a point, line, or plane that bisects the object

When you draw out a block on a grid that has been randomly changed, you will often get results that are not pleasing at all and that generally lack any sort of symmetry. Let's look at different types of symmetry in quilt blocks.

The type of symmetry that we commonly see in quilt blocks is symmetry on all sides. The common nine-patch is this type of block. All four corners are the same in both directions, and the center and middles are the same on all sides. The blocks mirror one side to the other both horizontally and vertically. Eight-pointed stars also fit in this category, as they are horizontally and vertically the same and the wedge from the center to the corner is the same on all sides. The following blocks are in this category.

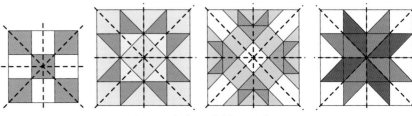

Symmetrical on all sides to others

Pinwheel, or spinning, symmetry occurs when the elements are the same but the direction in which the design faces rotates around the center. This is a very common arrangement of elements.

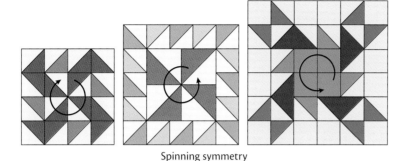

Spinning symmetry

Mirrored symmetry (bilateral) can be viewed three different ways—horizontally, vertically, or diagonally. Technically, if you put a mirror down the center of the design, the other side would appear correctly in the mirror, which means that half of the block is the mirror of the other half, but in only one direction. Blocks that are set on point are typical in this category, as are Basket blocks.

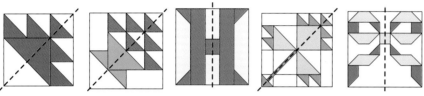

Bilateral mirrored symmetry

Double-mirrored symmetry is the same as bilateral symmetry, but it is a mirror of itself in two directions. It can be mirrored in both directions diagonally or can be the same both horizontally and vertically at the same time.

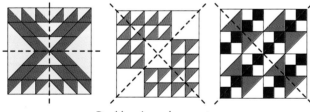

Double-mirrored symmetry

The next form of symmetry is more often found in settings with connector blocks than in actual block designs. We have included both. This is 180-degree rotation, which creates symmetry of the two units.

180-degree symmetry

Asymmetrical designs have no symmetry. Looking at the following blocks makes this category obvious.

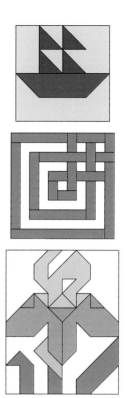

Asymmetrical

If these ideas have piqued your interest, keep going. What would you get if you experimented with any of these ideas in a setting with a linking block? With sashing? In a diagonal setting? With an internal frame? What if you made your pattern drawings with an unexpected symmetry? Can you see that the ideas you can come up with are endless with a bit of time and willingness to play and create? We hope you have enjoyed seeing how a simple process can create new and exciting designs.

Class 490

Borders with hexagons, stars, and diamonds

We include in this class a variety of borders that contain many of the elements that you have learned throughout this book. If you were diligent and worked through all the drafting lessons, we are confident that you can get a good start on working out the math needed to make these borders fit your projects. We are actually trying to whet your appetite for Volume 5, where we will address how to draft borders to fit the various stages of a quilt top as it evolves when you design your own medallion quilts (which is the topic for Volume 5). We did not add these borders to any of the projects in this book, as many of them appear too complex and heavy for the quilts we used for the lessons. But many of these borders would be spectacular if added to a simple design or used as a reflection of the quilt top that might use the same shapes and scale.

A border can draw the eye inward and reinforce the design of the overall quilt top, or it can be so busy that it competes with the interior design of the quilt top. There are a couple of approaches to finding out what will work best. One is to totally plan the quilt on paper, including the borders, to see if the scale and the complexity enhance or detract from the quilt top. The design, width, and number of fabrics are determined before cutting and sewing.

If the quilt top is finished, you can audition simple borders at the design wall. You can get a real feeling for the effects of the color, pattern, and placement of different fabrics on the overall look of the quilt. You may find that what looks good on paper does not always play out the same in the actual fabrics.

Determining the width of simple strip borders—either single or multiple—is easier when the quilt top is finished. As you audition different fabrics, you will see how their color and value play a part in how wide they need to be cut. It is hard to predetermine width until the border is next to the edge to which it will be added. You will also find that the fabrics used in the quilt top are not the only choices. Adding a totally new fabric can really pull a design together and add spark.

We have illustrated borders that contain elements of 60° and 45° diamonds, as well as hexagons and triangles. The entire block, or a combination of its parts, is repeated to make the border. Dissecting blocks to get various shapes that correspond with your vision of the quilt is a fun way to design an original border. We suggest that you go on a hunt for unique borders that inspire you by looking through books, magazines, and photos of all types of quilts. Start a file of ideas that will help jump-start a project later.

TIPS FOR PLANNING PIECED BORDERS

Here is a list of possible cures to compensate for differences between the size of the quilt top and the length of the desired border.

❋ When planning a pieced border, the easiest way to begin is to repeat units that are the same size as the quilt block or the individual units within the block.

Repeated elements from within quilt top

✳ Another approach is to add a small strip border to the edges of the quilt top before you add the pieced border. If the edges of the quilt top do not divide out evenly for the size of the units in the pieced border, this strip can add the additional length and width to accommodate the size of the pieced border. This is easier than trying to change the size of the pieced units.

✳ If you are using blocks that have pieces that interact and create new shapes when they are joined together, you can draw off these newly formed shapes. Draw four repeated blocks that represent the corner of the quilt. Draw units in the border area that complete the shapes on the outer edge of the blocks. The remaining space in the border can be left plain, or you can add more shapes as you like.

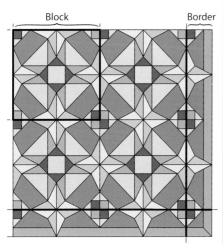
Block elements used to fill in spaces

✳ When the quilt top is not square, there may not be a number that works equally for both side and top and bottom measurements. A solution may be to add different-sized strips to the sides and the top and bottom of the quilt top. Look at Carrie's *Western Star* in Volume 3, Class 380 (page 102) for an example.

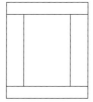
Different-sized strips for top and bottom

✳ As we did in the final quilt in Volume 3—*Goose in the Pond*—a diamond can be inserted in the center of each border to make Flying Geese fit. Adding a design element that relates to the pieces in the border but is a size that takes up the different space repeat, is one of the easiest methods for making borders fit.

Adding different element for spacer

✳ Spacers of background fabric added equally to either end of a pieced border are commonly seen on antique quilts. This is an easy way to add length to a short border.

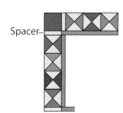
Adding spacer to ends of pieced border

✳ Corners can be troublesome. Not all designs turn corners easily. One solution is to add a pieced block that is separate from the border design. It can be related by using the same shapes in the border but in a different configuration.

Changing corner to pieced block

✳ Work on graph paper to plan border combinations that work within the scale of your quilt design. Work with different numbers of borders, adding a narrow strip border between different borders or changing the size of the grid or the number of repeats.

Changing grid sizes and/or adding strips

TIPS FOR PIECING PIECED BORDERS

✳ Accurate cutting, precise sewing, and well-honed ironing skills are needed to make great pieced borders. Handle the pieces carefully to avoid stretching edges that might not be on the straight grain.

✳ Measure and remeasure as you proceed with the border. Tiny adjustments can be made without showing if they are made equally as you go. If you wait until the entire border is pieced, it is usually obvious where the corrections are made. A tiny bit larger or smaller seam taken every once in a while is hardly noticeable, if at all.

✳ Even though we really push starch throughout all the projects, take it easy when pressing borders. If the seams and fabric are set with starch, it can be hard to ease the border onto the quilt top if needed.

✳ Pins are critical to placing the border on the edge equally. Distribute any fullness equally along the entire edge.

❈ Pieced borders that are on the far outside edge of the quilt can be very difficult to keep straight. If your design allows, add a straight strip border on the outermost edge or, at the very least, keep the straight grain on the outside edge of each pieced unit.

Following is a gallery of pieced borders using 60° and 45° diamonds, as well as hexagons and triangles. We have included simple to complicated designs. Can you come up with any more? Can you create different corners?

60° ANGLES

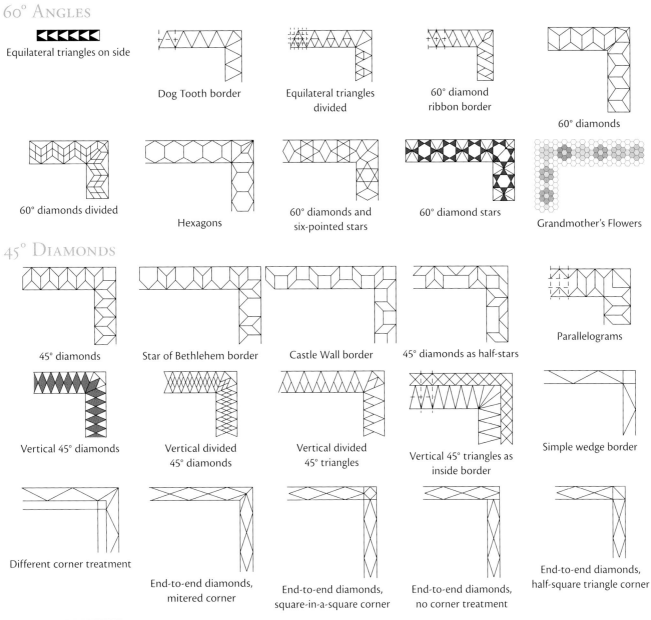

Equilateral triangles on side

Dog Tooth border

Equilateral triangles divided

60° diamond ribbon border

60° diamonds

60° diamonds divided

Hexagons

60° diamonds and six-pointed stars

60° diamond stars

Grandmother's Flowers

45° DIAMONDS

45° diamonds

Star of Bethlehem border

Castle Wall border

45° diamonds as half-stars

Parallelograms

Vertical 45° diamonds

Vertical divided 45° diamonds

Vertical divided 45° triangles

Vertical 45° triangles as inside border

Simple wedge border

Different corner treatment

End-to-end diamonds, mitered corner

End-to-end diamonds, square-in-a-square corner

End-to-end diamonds, no corner treatment

End-to-end diamonds, half-square triangle corner

Diamonds among diamonds

LESSON TWO:

Making bias binding

We find that when we are manipulating binding around tight inside and outside corners, bias binding is more pliable and easier to work with. You might want to make a sample to determine the width of binding you desire on your chosen project. As you have learned in the previous volumes of *Quilter's Academy*, we use a narrower binding than is the general rule. The reason for this is the thickness of the batting. Back in the 1980s when we used thick, fluffy polyester batting, the binding needed to be cut 2½″ to accommodate the thickness of the batting and to cover the wider seam allowances that we sewed with then. Now that we sew with narrower seams and our batting is very thin, the binding needs to be cut narrower to give a good sharp edge and to have the binding completely full. If the binding doesn't cover the edge of the batting tightly, the edge will not wear well and will have a sloppy appearance.

Wallhanging (36″ × 36″)	4 strips × 1¾″ wide = 7″	¼ yard
Twin (54″ × 90″)	8 strips × 1¾″ wide = 14″	⅜ yard
Full (72″ × 90″)	8 strips × 1¾″ wide = 14″	⅜ yard
Queen (90″ × 108″)	10 strips × 1¾″ wide = 18″	½ yard
King (120″ × 120″)	12 strips × 1¾″ wide = 21″	⅝ yard

BINDING WIDTHS

When making bias binding, the easiest way is to use the continuous method. The following chart will help you determine how big to cut your square based on the amount of binding needed.

1. Cut a square of fabric the size needed. Cut the square in half diagonally, creating 2 triangles.

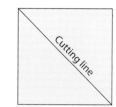

Cutting square in half diagonally

2. Sew these triangles together, as shown, with a ¼″ seam.

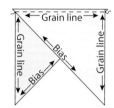

Sewing 2 triangles together

3. After sewing, open the triangles and press the seam open. This will give you a parallelogram. Using a ruler, mark the entire backside with lines spaced the width you need to cut your bias. Cut on the first line about 5″.

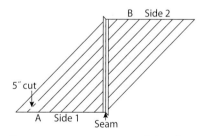

Press seam open, measure, and draw lines

4. Connect A and B and side 1 and side 2 to form a tube. (The cut edge on the first line will line up with the raw edge at B. This will allow the first

line to be offset by a line). Pin the raw ends together, making sure that the lines match. Sew with a ¼″ seam allowance.

Offset by one line and sew tube.

If you have aligned the seam properly, you will have an extra strip at each end. Continue cutting on the line you started in Step 3. As you cut on the line, the tube will become one long continuous piece of bias binding.

Once you have cut all the lines, press the binding in half and starch lightly. At the cutting mat, use your ruler to measure from the folded edge and trim the raw edges to create a very straight and accurate binding. This will give you a very straight finished binding.

Here is an easy formula for figuring the size square you need for the required length of bias: Divide the square size by the width of your bias and then multiply only the whole number of the answer by the square size again. Example: a 22″ square divided by 1¾″ (width of cut bias) = 12.57. Multiply 12 by 22″ = 264″ of continuous bias yielded. If you need this in yardage, divide by 36.

Wallhanging	36″ × 36″ + 12 = 156″	18″ ÷ 1.75″ = 10 × 18″ = 180″	18″ square
Twin	54″ × 90″ + 12 = 300″	24″ ÷ 1.75″ = 13 × 24″ = 312″	24″ square
Full	72″ × 90″ + 12 = 336″	26″ ÷ 1.75″ = 14 × 26″ = 364″	26″ square
Queen	90″ × 108″ + 12 = 408″	28″ ÷ 1.75″ = 16 × 28″ = 448″	28″ square
King	120″ × 120″ + 12 = 492″	30″ ÷ 1.75″ = 17 × 30″ = 510″	30″ square

Obviously, these yardages are for straight-sided quilts. If you are planning to bind the outside edges of hexagons or other uneven edges, you will need to actually measure how much binding is needed for each hexagon and multiply that by how many hexagons you will be binding. Be sure to add quite a bit of extra to allow for the many turns—both inside and out.

Finishing the edges of inside corners and points

Binding quilts with inside and 60° corners requires a different process than binding 90° corners. Hexagon designs can be handled in a couple of different ways. The easiest way is to cut through the last round of hexagon pieces to create a straight edge. This often causes you to cut through a block, such as Grandmother's Flower Garden or Pinwheel; so you will need to decide how much work you want to put into the edge finish. Designs such as Carrie's *Mosaic Star* table topper, from Class 410 (page 18), lend themselves to cutting a straight edge without disturbing the design. If you want to retain the shapes, you can face the edge, fold in the seam allowances and do a knife-edge, or do an actual binding.

FACING

A facing is a nice finish for irregular edges. If you do not want to cut through the blocks or pieces to get a straight edge, but you also do not want to bind every little hexagon, a facing might be the answer. A facing is also a clean finish on a quilt for which a binding would add bulk or a stripe that you do not desire. The final border is the actual edge of the quilt. This is not a durable finish, so take that into account if the quilt is going to be used on a bed or as a throw. Also take into consideration the color of the facing, as you will see the very edge of it at the seam on the edge of the quilt.

If the quilt is small, it is easiest to use a piece of fabric that is the size of the quilt, cutting away the interior of the fabric. This creates a piece of facing without any seams. It does take quite a bit of fabric, but if your quilt is an irregular shape, this is much easier than trying to join strips at odd angles at each corner. It also eliminates bulky seams.

When removing the center of the fabric, leave enough so that the facing is wide enough to extend beyond the deepest point of the edge plus 1″–2″.

Trimmed quilt top

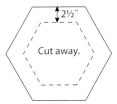

Use solid piece of fabric for facing small quilts.

If you are facing a larger quilt and do not want to waste so much fabric, make the facing from strips sewn together to accommodate your measurements. Cut the facing at least 2½″ wide. Cut the strips for the top and bottom of the quilt

the width measurement. Cut the side strips the length of the quilt minus the top and bottom widths plus 1″ for seam allowances. Once all four pieces are joined, press the seam allowances open. The corners will be cleaned up when the you hand sew at the end.

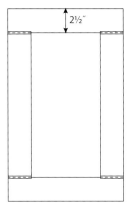

Sewing strips together for facing larger quilts

Before adding the facing, carefully trim the edges of the quilt exactly along each side of each shape. To sew the facing onto the quilt, position it on the right side of the quilt top, right sides together. Pin or baste to hold in place. You will be sewing from the backside, where you can see and guide along the edge. You will be stitching from dot to dot along each edge. If you can't see the dots marked for the piecing, you might want to add dots at each pivot point for accuracy.

Begin stitching. As you approach each pivot point, shorten your stitches to add strength to the corners when the facing is turned. Stitch around the entire quilt.

Trim the seam allowances to ⅛″, making a clip at each inside point and trimming away most of the excess seam allowance on the outside points. This will give you a sharper point by eliminating the bulk and will allow the batting to form a miter inside the turned edge.

Turn the facing to the back, carefully pushing out the outside corners. Using a point turner to gently create the points is very helpful. Take your time and work carefully. This is not a quick process.

Turning point with point turner

As you turn the points, pin in place. Every once in a while, go to the ironing board and press the edge flat. Once all of the edges are turned, turn under the raw edge to establish a straight and even measurement from the inside points; hand stitch the folded edge in place.

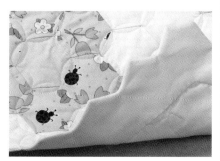
Finished edge—front and back

KNIFE-EDGE

note *Choose the type of binding you want to use before quilting the top. If you are going to use the knife-edge finish, do not quilt the outside edge of the hexagons or other shapes. You need to have access to the layers for trimming and turning the edges.*

Another method to finish these edges is to turn in the edges of both the back and front and whipstitch the edge. The batting needs to be trimmed to the seamline. Turn the top edge over the trimmed batting edge and baste. Turn the backing in to match the folded edge of the top. You may also need to baste or press this edge to make it easier to stitch. Hand stitch with matching thread, using tiny overcast stitches.

Close-up of knife-edge finish

tip You might want to take the time to stitch ¼″ from the raw edge of each hexagon before layering and quilting the top. This will give you a guide to turn and press the seam allowance before trimming the batting. Trim the batting just a bit shorter than the folded edge and then tuck the batting into the folded hexagon.

BINDING

If you have trimmed the sides of a hexagon quilt to straight edges, you may still encounter 60° corners. These are handled in the same manner as a square corner, but the turn is not a true miter. The process is the same but with a small adjustment.

If you are binding many inside and outside corners, be patient. There is a lot of turning and mitering involved.

Start the process by sewing a line of stitching, just a thread narrower

than your seam allowance, around all the edges of the quilt. Make a small clip straight from the edge to the inside point, stopping just shy of the stitching. This will allow you to straighten the edge as you apply the binding.

Clipping inside corners

You will find that binding a complex edge like this is easier with narrow binding. We cut our bias strips ⅞″ wide, using a single thickness. This gives a ³⁄₁₆″ finished binding.

note *We use a single-thickness binding, as a double-fold binding is a bit bulky and stiff to work with. It is also very difficult to work with a double-fold binding when you want to create an edge this small. We suggest you make a couple of samples before beginning, as binding this type of edge is a very labor-intensive process, and you want to really like it in the end.*

Side-by-side bindings—double fold (right) and single fold (left)

Start sewing the binding onto the edge. Be sure to leave about 8″–10″ at the beginning and start the sewing on an outside straight edge, if possible. Sew toward the first inside point and stop with your needle in the down position, using a seam allowance slightly wider than ⅛".

Stop right at intersection.

Turn quilt to create straight edge.

With the needle still in the fabric, lift the presser foot and pull the edge straight behind the needle so that you create a straight edge. If you have a knee lift for your presser foot, this is a perfect place to use it. The clip that you made will allow the edge to straighten. Continue sewing. Notice that there is no miter here and that the binding is standing straight up. The miter will be formed when you hand stitch the binding into place.

Once you get to the outside corner, stop stitching at the seamline, turn the quilt, and backstitch off the edge, making sure you stay at the same angle as the raw edge on the right. You will not be stitching straight but at the 60°angle. Pull the quilt away from the needle and fold the binding up. Fold the binding over itself at the corner and align the raw edge of the binding and the edge of the quilt. This is exactly how you miter a square corner—but unlike a square corner, where all the edges align with each other, this time the binding will not align with the top edge of the quilt.

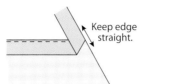

Turning 60° corner

Turning 60° corner

Once you have been around all sides of the quilt, join the ends using either of the methods covered in Volumes 1 and 2, or your method of choice. Trim all the layers if necessary to keep the seam allowance exactly the same width. Turn the binding to the back, fold over the seam allowance, and align the folded edge with the seam. Hand stitch, using either a blind or a ladder stitch.

LESSON FOUR:
Quilting designs (17 quilts and/or projects)

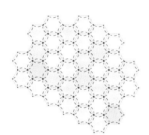

Teatime design

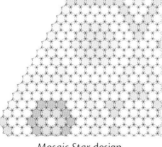

Mosaic Star design

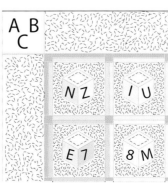

Tumbling Block design

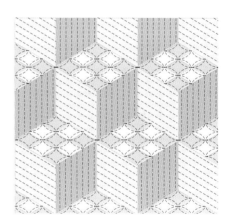

Blue Stairs to Heaven design

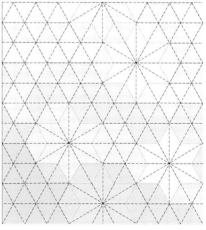

Constellation design

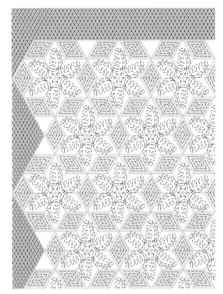

French Boutonnière design

Diamond Starburst design

Spring Garden design

Shop Hop design

Stars Aplenty design

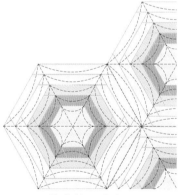

Bird's Nests design

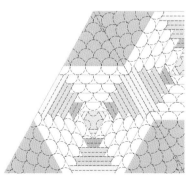

Pineapples All Around design

Prayer Star design

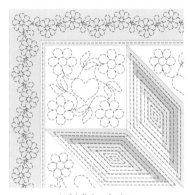

Whirligigs design

Pinwheel design

Amish Pastures design

Senior Final

We are approaching your final differently in this volume. We remember our senior years in college, with our favorite part being independent study and lab classes. The end of the senior year was a time when we could venture out on our own, pursue our own tastes and style, and apply everything we had learned throughout the four years of college.

Harriet spent her senior year designing and making all the garments in her entire wedding party, including the mothers' dresses and her future husband's sport jacket, which he wore after the wedding. These projects put into practical use all the classes that she took—her drafting, flat pattern, draping, tailoring, and fashion design classes, as well as planning the wedding using all the other classes offered while procuring her degree in home economics.

Carrie, on the other hand, had four senior years as she worked to obtain her two bachelor's degrees in wildlife biology and range management. Carrie was on a path to work for the Bureau of Land Management and ranchers. She spent those years learning to castrate baby pigs and bulls, milk cows, and plan and design grazing systems for ranchers. She spent the majority of her time out in the field or in lab classes. There she had to put to work all that she had learned in her previous years of schooling to come up with solutions to problems presented in real-life situations on a working ranch or wildlife preserve area.

This is what we are challenging you to think about and do. If you have worked through all four volumes of *Quilter's Academy,* you have an amazing amount of information, knowledge, and experience under your belt. We realize that for the majority of our readers, this is a self-directed home study course, and we imagine most did not do all the classes or lessons. However, if you did, your mind should be eager to go on to designing original designs. Do not let complexity slow you down. Upon completing your senior year work through this book, your skills are up to the challenge.

We would love for you to share your creations with us, as well as with our followers. Please email photos for us to use at the address in Resources (page 128), or post them on our Quilter's Academy blog.

We are diving into Volume 5 as soon as this is sent off to the publisher, and we are more than excited about the quilts that are going to come out of teaching you to draft and design your own medallion quilts. We also have lots of ideas for the PhD year, so keep up the good work. Just think of all you have accomplished up to now!

About the Authors

Harriet started quilting seriously in 1974, working alongside her mom. Her early quilting career included producing baby quilts for craft shows and teaching adult education classes. In 1981, Harriet opened her quilt shop, Harriet's Treadle Arts. Her specialties at the time were free-motion embroidery, machine arts, and machine quilting.

In 1982, Harriet attended one of Mary Ellen Hopkins's seminars. Mary Ellen's streamlined techniques and innovative design ideas led Harriet to a new way of thinking, which caused her to give up the machine arts and to teach only quilting. Today, she is world renowned for being a true "mover and shaker" in the quilt world.

In the late 1990s, she was voted one of the "88 Leaders of the Quilt World."

Harriet created and inspired a whole new generation of machine quilters with her best-selling book *Heirloom Machine Quilting,* which has enjoyed 22 continuous years in print. She is also the author of *Mastering Machine Appliqué* and *From Fiber to Fabric,* and co-author of *The Art of Classic Quiltmaking.* She is responsible for a myriad of products pertaining to machine quilting, and she has developed batting with Hobbs Bonded Fibers and designed fabric for P&B Textiles.

Carrie has been around quilting all her life—sitting in Harriet's lap as a baby while Harriet sewed, learning her colors with machine embroidery thread and her alphabet on the cams of Harriet's old Viking sewing machine. She didn't have a chance not to be involved! Harriet and her mother opened the store when Carrie was four years old, and Carrie spent a part of nearly every day of her life at the store. Carrie's interests in college turned to range management and wildlife biology, but no

matter what, she always came home to quilting as a hobby.

In 2006, Harriet decided she wanted to close the store. She was tired after running it for 25 years, as well as traveling and teaching at the same time. Carrie couldn't imagine not having the store as a part of her life. So she moved back to Colorado and now runs the store full time.

Most of all, Carrie is proud to carry on the family legacy of quilting that extends from her great-great-grandmother Phoebie Frazier to her great-grandmother Harriet Carey to her grandmother Harriet (Fran) Frazier to her mom, Harriet. Quilting is all about tradition (no matter how you make a quilt) and about the love of creating something beautiful from fabric and thread with your own hands.

All the quilts in the book were pieced and quilted by Harriet and Carrie. They truly believe that if you are going to teach it, you had better be able to make it!

Resources

SUPPLIES/ SOURCE LIST

All notions and supplies referred to in the text are available from the following:

Harriet's Treadle Arts
6390 West 44th Avenue
Wheat Ridge, CO 80033
303-424-2742
harrietstreadlearts@earthlink.net
www.harriethargrave.com

Information on Harriet's classes, retreats, and conferences can be found on her website.

If you are looking for copies of Harriet's out-of-print books referred to in the text, they are available through C&T as eBooks and as POD (Print-On-Demand) Editions. Go to www.ctpub.com and search by author name to purchase.

Other titles by Harriet Hargrave: